IF THE FIRST LADY HIRED ME...

A Private Eye's Tell-All on Cheating in America

JUSTIN HOPSON

Copyright © 2018 Justin Hopson.

P.O. Box 1965
Charleston, SC 29465

All rights reserved. No part of this book may be reproduced, stored, or transmitted by any means—whether auditory, graphic, mechanical, or electronic—without written permission of the author, except in the case of brief excerpts used in critical articles and reviews. Unauthorized reproduction of any part of this work is illegal and is punishable by law.

Author photo by Merideth Garrigan (A Spot in Time Photography).

THE HOLY BIBLE, NEW INTERNATIONAL VERSION®, NIV® Copyright © 1973, 1978, 1984, 2011 by Biblica, Inc.® Used by permission. All rights reserved worldwide.

This book is a work of non-fiction. Unless otherwise noted, the author and the publisher make no explicit guarantees as to the accuracy of the information contained in this book and in some cases, names of people and places have been altered to protect their privacy.

ISBN: 978-1-7323198-2-0 (sc)
ISBN: 978-1-7323198-9-9 (hc)
ISBN: 978-1-7323198-4-4 (e)
ISBN: 978-1-7323198-8-2 (audio)

Because of the dynamic nature of the Internet, any web addresses or links contained in this book may have changed since publication and may no longer be valid. The views expressed in this work are solely those of the author and do not necessarily reflect the views of the publisher, and the publisher hereby disclaims any responsibility for them.

Any people depicted in stock imagery provided by Getty Images are models, and such images are being used for illustrative purposes only.
Certain stock imagery © Getty Images.

rev. date: 01/29/2019

"What price cheating? Justin Hopson's "If the First Lady Hired Me…" answers that loaded question in his book that is both a how-to about hiring a private investigator and a thrilling tell-all of case histories. If the First Lady Hired Me…is both riveting and disquieting. A must-read for anyone who suspects cheating. I couldn't put it down."
Mary Alice Monroe, New York Times bestselling novelist

"The more people that rationalize cheating, the more it becomes a culture of dishonesty. And that can become a vicious downward cycle. Because suddenly, if everyone else is cheating, you feel the need to cheat, too." ~ Stephen Covey

Acknowledgments

First and foremost, all glory to God, my Shepherd. My appreciation abounds for my wife and children, who have been and always will be my emotional backbone. Endless gratitude goes to my friends and family, whose unwavering support is the wind in my sails. Thank you, thank you, thank you to Diane DiLorenzo, David L. Savage, Frank Serpico, John Oliva, Stefano Randazzo, Elizabeth Lee Beck, and Julian Assange for sending inspiration my way. Two thumbs-up for the collaborative efforts of Rob Suggs—for being part of the marrow of this book. Cover photo credit to the talented, Glenn Francis. Last but not least, a shout out goes to my fellow private investigators both near and far…stay focused and keep up the good work.

Disclaimer

This book, in its entirety, is a fact-based personal account, with the sole exception of altered names and occupations in a few cases to protect personal privacy. Please be advised that these pages do not condone ill will or harm towards Donald Trump. To the best of my knowledge, the data collected for all exhibits was obtained through investigative reports, court records, police reports, print media, and social media. Facts and testimony can be verified through Hopson v. State of New Jersey, et al (Case #1:03-cv-5817). All copy-written material has been permitted.

Contents

Acknowledgments vii
Disclaimer ix
Foreword xiii

Chapter 1   No Limit 1
Chapter 2   How Would I Know? 13
Chapter 3   Private Eye 101 20
Chapter 4   Love Thy Neighbor 28
Chapter 5   You Do the Math 37
Chapter 6   Lovesick to Lost Love 45
Chapter 7   United States of ~~America~~ Entertainment 59
Chapter 8   First Lady, We Need to Talk… 70
Chapter 9   The Case Against Donald Trump 76
Chapter 10 Cheat and Repeat 88
Chapter 11 Divine Intervention 94
Chapter 12 Trump vs. Trump 101
Chapter 13 Cheating is the Kiss of Death… 110

Foreword

On April 21, 2018, I received an email from a Justin Hopson, which said in part:

> As a ... private investigator and retired New Jersey State Trooper, I've been following the Trump allegations very closely. Consequently, I am writing a narrative nonfiction book ... *A Private Eye's Tell-All on Cheating in America*. I am reaching out to respectfully ask if you'd be willing to write a short forward for my book...

Upon further reading up about Justin and his life path so far, I realized that he is a rare bird. Rare in that he is uncompromising with his actions when it comes to matters dictated to him by his inner voice, regardless of what authority figures order him to do, and obstinate in his moral conclusions, regardless of the personal gain and comfort that may come his way if he just tamped down on that quiet voice that he calls his "conscience" in Chapter 7. Perhaps we need more people like Mr. Hopson throughout the fabric of our society, and the fact that someone like him strikes me as "rare" is the problem.

I told him I would be happy to write a foreword for his book. He then emailed me a confidential galley proof, and thus began my literary entry into the world of private surveillance, divorces, and literally, sex, lies, and videotapes.

This was a fascinating read for me, because although I am an attorney, I do not practice family law, a subspecialty in law. I have had my fair share of high-profile cases, but the world of divorces is a different animal indeed. It is profoundly personal for those involved, and ropes in innocent bystanders, leaving them scarred, to an extent that civil cases generally do not.

· · · · · · · · · · ● · · · · · · · · · · ·

Mr. Hopson's book presents, in the context of marital infidelity, a choice that faces all of us in one way or another as we each go through this short sojourn on earth.

The choice is: can I do something simply because it is LEGAL? Does "legality" give me *carte blanche* cover to do as I please?

Posited in a slightly different way, the choice can be: if I can get away with "it," should I do "it"?

Now, "it" can be many things. In this book, "it" is marital infidelity, or, as Mr. Hopson puts it bluntly, "cheating."

· · · · · · · · · · ● · · · · · · · · · · ·

However, as Mr. Hopson's quote about cheaters, attributed to Andrew Keane, shows, we continue to hold on to this idea that "cheating" is wrong, and should not lead to reward.

Mr. Hopson, through his narrations of his professional life as a private investigator, gives examples of the fallout that occurs when people cheat. In a few examples, he goes into gory detail. The gory details not only describe what he is seeing and hearing as a modern-day gumshoe hiding behind restaurant menus and garbage bins, but also what happens when the cheaters get caught. As anyone who has been in an intimate, trusting relationship can imagine, the fallout is tremendous.

None of this fall into "legality." It is NOT illegal to break your spouse's heart and rend your family apart. Heck, you may even get away with "it" for years.

How is it wrong, if it is not "illegal"? Mr. Hopson states that it is a moral issue. He "make[s] no judgments on the politics; what [he is] concerned about here is the message about morality." Chapter 1. According to Hopson, "It's a matter of human discipline, morality." Chapter 10.

• • • • • • • • • ● • • • • • • • • • •

Mr. Hopson couches his message as one directed to Ms. Melania Trump, our current First Lady. Her husband Donald Trump, the current President of the United States, is thrice-married, with children from each marriage. He has admitted to numerous extramarital affairs. None of this is illegal; he is presumably financially supporting all his many issue; but it sets a moral tone for the entire country.

It is interesting that this book is not a fire-and-brimstone diatribe against those who choose to cheat. I believe Mr. Hopson is too practical for that. Instead, it holds his professional observations from the trenches after a career in private investigation work after he fled his job as a New Jersey State Trooper (you can read his memoir about this in his previous book, *Breaking the Blue Wall: One Man's War Against Police Corruption*).

He is deferential in his message to Ms. Trump, First Lady, but my takeaway is: perhaps it is up to all of us to rein in the cheaters, and stop enabling their behavior, regardless of any perceived immediate personal cost and suffering. And those who can do this best are those closest to the transgressors. Only then can we get back on the right track as a country that answers NO to both my questions presented above.

Elizabeth Lee Beck, Esq.

May 15, 2018

CHAPTER 1
No Limit

"If a picture is worth a thousand words, then a surveillance video is worth ten thousand thoughts."
Justin Hopson

I closely watched as he shut the door behind them. He turned quickly and reached for her. The festivities were underway.

He took hold of her by the hips and pulled her into a tight embrace.

It was then that I saw his hands explore her body, lingering on her neck and down to her breasts. His left hand bore a gold wedding ring. If she noticed, it wasn't news, or perhaps she just didn't care. Like him, she was fully immersed in desire and gaining distance from ordinary inhibitions. Wearing a seductive smile, her lips inched towards his ear and whispered words of passion. Desire and endorphins were seizing center stage.

More and more, he expressed his appetite in a show of dominance. He squeezed her neck, she gasped, and her head snapped backward. Her long, brown hair fanned outward against the wall. She cracked a smile, biting her lip, as he squeezed even harder; I focus in on her arousal at the violence of his hands.

I then moved a few inches, changing my view, as the young vixen gripped the edge of the sofa and circled him. Closing her eyes, she let it all happen—his lips, moving to her neck and then below; his hands ripping at her blouse. In kind, she quickly began unbuttoning his fitted designer shirt.

Her fingernails now dug into and scratched his chest as she took control, pushing him toward the sofa.

I assumed the motive behind the scratch was twofold: first, a message to the man's wife and second an expression of jealousy to the recipient— she didn't want to share him. Whatever the case, her animal impulses were in full rage. The two of them continued to kiss every inch of either other, to explore, to scratch, even as the phone began ringing. The sound could be taken as an omen of warning, but it was too late for that. The couple just ignored it, their mutual desire angry enough that it must be quenched, regardless of consequence.

I checked my watch.

By now, their clothes, in disarray or even tatters, were discarded and forgotten. He reached for her in the most intimate of ways and places, and she did the same. The foreplay itself might be a hard act to follow when the main event finally arrived.

I checked the camera, making sure the lighting and focus were on point and then double-checking the accuracy of the time stamp. It's the surveillance camera that untangles the web of deception spun by a cheater, and it's the private eye who is the firsthand witness to the cover up, which is often worse than the crime. I was filming for documentation purposes, not pornography, but it was essential to get the details recorded. As the lovers pursued every other part of the body, I cared mostly about the two faces. If they didn't come through visibly, I'd be wasting my time.

With a gust of wind, the sheer white curtains lifted momentarily. The sliding glass door was open, and if either of them hadn't been so utterly distracted, they wouldn't have been so careless. Their misstep allowed me to film their every intimate move.

But she only had eyes for him, and he for her. Such is human passion. She took his hand, leading him to a table where the main course would be served. She struck a seductive pose—superfluous, of course, at this point— smiling coyly at him over her shoulder. He approached her from behind, and she reached down to guide him.

Once they were involved, I might as well have stepped into the room for a close-up without their noticing. Hell, I wouldn't have even had to be particularly quiet—they were making enough primal sound to provide cover.

Not that any private eye would ever do anything so reckless.

Once more he took the lead, once more the aggressor as he flipped her body around and pushed her down flush against the tabletop. She cried out while they continued to work out the physicality of their adulterous affair.

Finally, given the limitations of human energy, the encounter came to a panting conclusion. They lay quietly for a few minutes...then strolled together onto the balcony for a smoke. He checked his phone as she took a drag from the cigarette they were sharing.

The vixen stood behind him, enclosing his shoulders with her arms in a gesture both sensual and, I noticed, stealthy: she was interested in seeing the screen name on his phone.

Both played the game. She pretended not to have seen while he pretended not to have concealed. The phone disappeared into the shirt, he continued buttoning, and she took another long, thoughtful drag. I could only wonder what she, the paramour, was thinking.

He pulled up his pants and socks and laced his shoes, taking far more care than he'd shown during the festivities.

The man, whose name was Hicks, gave her a brief kiss—again, more casual this time—and left the condo through the front door. I kept the camera running, capturing the way he adjusted his collar just so, the way he ran his fingers through his curly, clean-cut hair with apparent satisfaction. This was the body language of a man who was pleased with himself. He'd placed his order, and it had been served precisely to his taste.

I thought about Hicks's wife and his twin daughters as he climbed into his late model silver Mercedes and turned the key in the ignition. Alyssa leaned against the door of the condo and drank in his every movement with her eyes. Her captivation with Hicks was only too clear.

The Mercedes had a vanity tag—"NOLIMIT"—and I managed to focus the camera on it and get a good shot of the car driving away. I made sure the date and time were recorded and knew I'd succeeded in recording vital evidence of a crucial reality.

A pile of leaves kept me out of sight. I stood up from behind the HVAC compressor and brushed away the dust and loose grass, quickly returning the camera to its case. I shook away as much grit as possible. A warm shower was going to feel good.

Filming without being spotted isn't an unattainable goal, but you have to be good at it. You need a firm understanding of people and how they think, what they're likely to notice. Also important is the ability to think outside the box and as I have mentioned—outwit your target. A private eye chasing a cheater is the ultimate game of cat and mouse. But a botched mission could lead to any number of unwanted results; including physical violence...I'd like to think that I'd be ready for that too.

Best to keep it simple and get in and out invisibly.

I gathered the high-definition video camera, night vision scope, and hurried to my car—snugly parked at a safe distance—and prepared to follow the real-time GPS tracking device I'd placed on the Mercedes. The beauty of a tracking device is that I don't need line of sight at every moment. So I had time for a quick text message to my client, Mrs. Hicks. "Husband home in 8 min." I then sent the text.

This, of course, triggered a series of anxious phone calls from her. All in human nature, completely understandable, but I was going to tell her as little as possible.

A client must be managed as carefully as a target. Every action has an equal and opposite reaction. If Mrs. Hicks knew exactly what had occurred that night, the predictable emotions would come into play, and one of two things would happen. The first might be a crime of passion, dropping me in the middle of an assault or manslaughter case. The second might be a verbal confrontation—*"Who is she? Yes, I know about her! What's her name?"* Either way, my investigation would come to a quick conclusion, before I completed my evidence gathering.

There would be a time and a place for sharing the facts and the evidence with my client. But not quite yet.

• • • • • • • • ● • • • • • • • • •

Two days later, I briefly met Mrs. Hicks and suggested this would be a good time to take her kids on a weekend getaway. This seemed like an odd suggestion to her, so she said, "What? Why would I do that?"

"On the theory that your husband is having an affair—let's say it's true—we need to give him an opportunity to show us. Out of town with the kids, you make it easy on him. So my suggestion is for you to cast a long fishing line, by letting your husband know the three of you are somewhere out of the way, and meanwhile I'll set the hook."

Mrs. Hicks was silent for a moment, thinking as if these words made everything real for the first time. Maybe it was actually happening—her husband cheating on her.

"Do you think he's—do you think he's doing that? Having an affair?" she asked.

I answered, "It's more likely than not."

She looked down at the wedding ring on her finger for a moment, reflected, and said, "All right. I'll do it. My parents live about three hours away, and they love to see their grandchildren. We'll go see them this weekend. And you'll—"

"I'll take care of the rest. Don't worry about anything."

The meeting ended after she mentioned, "I wish it were that easy, Justin."

A few days later, I rented a white compact car; ordinary, innocuous. I drove it on a few dirt roads to give it a nice, dusty coating. Rental cars are noticed by the suspicious if they're sharp. I placed a box of tissue on the dash, pushed down the sun visors, and hung a handful of air fresheners on the rearview mirror. The purpose of all these was to obstruct visibility into my car. From any angle, it would be tough to get any glimpse of my face.

All my electronics were in the backseat, so I placed an infant car seat and blanket back there to confuse the issue for anyone peeking in. A snoop wouldn't be toting babies around.

Prior to that weekend, I conducted a background check on Hicks' paramour, Alyssa. It turns out that she was squeaky clean other than having an insatiable appetite for a married man. Mr. Hicks' past was another story that I'll disclose later...

There continues to be one nice development when chasing cheaters. Two-timers are making it a little easier on people like me, by leaving a thick trail of social media. I'd hate to do this job without the way they document their own lives to the world. Mr. Hicks and I, it had turned out, had a mutual friend, who was helping me monitor Mr. Hicks online. I also had access to Mr. Hicks's e-mail.

Putting all these tidbits together, I learned Hicks planned to spend the weekend with Alyssa and was starting to get a picture of why the back of his car said, "NOLIMITS."

I'd soon have his phone records as well, but that would take another week. In time, however, most information surfaces somehow.

Friday afternoon arrived. Hicks took off from work a bit early, and I pulled out of my parking spot casually. I followed him a few cars back as he left the lot. He headed for a nearby carwash and gave his Mercedes a thorough bath. Next, sparkling clean, Hicks headed for a liquor store for adult beverages and cigarettes.

Following him was a bit of a challenge. Whether he was excited or just a lousy driver, Hicks threaded his way through traffic to finally reach a popular steakhouse franchise. The car door opened, he slid out, and he stood, slowly panning the perimeter with his eyes. Had he made me? For just a second, I caught my breath.

Then he whirled as Alyssa appeared from behind to plant a kiss on his neck. He'd been looking for her; my nerves abated. For the time being, anyway.

I sat in the car and gave the couple a few minutes to get their table and settle in. Then I entered the restaurant, and there was Hicks, not far away. I was careful to avoid eye contact. He sat at the bar with a beer in his hand, and he was facing away from me - caught up in conversation with Alyssa. A casual glance informed me that an appetizer plate was between them. This meant they were eating at the bar.

The hostess wanted to seat me. I took the wine list from her, moved around her, and said, "I'd love to sit right here," indicating a table. "Is that okay?"

"Um, sure."

The booth was just within earshot of my targets. I stood the wine menu upright on the table, my hands within. I scratched my left hand casually, and the micro-camera slid neatly from my right sleeve into the left palm—all while I pretended to make an informed wine choice.

The recent sexual romp had been all action, almost no energy wasted on talk. This time I could hear the conversation and get more of a sense of the personalities I was dealing with. I fought a smile. These two were bantering back and forth like two high school sweethearts. It was a vast distance from the vicious "adult" display I'd filmed at the condo.

As they chatted, I learned that the affair was about a month old. Adolescent-level teasing went back and forth. He'd brush her thigh with his fingers—just a little too close—while making his point. She'd raise an eyebrow, slightly turn her face, and strike a pouty expression in response.

He leaned in to whisper some secret, though it was clearly along the theme of how badly he wanted her right that moment. As with many affairs of this type, the two of them were living out their own B-movie. I could also read their lips here and there, and he seemed to be letting her know he had a surprise in store. In the course of all this, he punctuated the discussion with three beers and a shot of something stronger.

I was so focused on what was happening at the bar that I didn't hear the waiter immediately. He brought my order of barbecue shrimp with tequila on the rocks.

"Can I take your wine list?" he asked.

"No, I'll keep it, if you don't mind. I might still order a glass of red. But could you go ahead and bring me the check?"

The waiter looked a bit confused, but nodded, smiled politely, and departed. The hostess may have told him the guy at this table does things his way. The point was I needed to be able to pay and leave on quick notice.

I recorded, as well as I could, the conversation at the bar, but it was going to be a very muffled sound file. Bars are noisy—terrible for this kind of thing. Pictures and sounds of touching and flirting helped paint a picture, but the evidence that counted was the kind of thing I'd filmed at the condo.

People are surprised to learn that adultery is still on the books as illegal in twenty-one states, though typically handled as a misdemeanor and rarely prosecuted. Still, video evidence has an impact once you get to the courtroom, in both civil and criminal cases. One small video file, provided the two faces are identifiable, is damning evidence.

I knew Hicks and Alyssa wouldn't linger all night in this place—not after all that seductive interplay. When the waiter finally brought Hicks the check, I left cash on my table and left a few steps behind them, making a good show of being in no particular hurry.

I climbed into my dusty rental car, adjusted my various cameras for night conditions, and waited to pull out of the lot comfortably behind the couple. The twist was that they were in Alyssa's car, due to the three beers and the shot he'd put down. This made my GPS tracking device useless;

Hicks was a few drinks in that direction himself, though I imagined she would still find various uses for him before the night was over.

She drove him into the city, making it difficult for me to keep within safe distance without losing them. Downtown was lively that night, and she couldn't seem to find a place to park. I wondered what direction their conversation was taking. She gave up on a parking spot, headed for a nearby suburb, and after hovering here and there, pulled into a lot of an abandoned food market. I kept driving, circled the block, and found an adjacent lot with suitable sight lines. I, too, pulled in and waited.

Alyssa's car didn't park in front of the market. She moved again, steering into an alleyway behind the building, a private place. I imagined they'd be parked for a while. So I grabbed my cameras and began quietly making my way toward the alleyway, staying out of the glare of street lights.

Near the wall, I found an old dumpster, a workable spot for my surveillance efforts. With a great deal of stealth, I approached it. Thirty feet or so away, I could see the headlights of Alyssa's car dimming as they parked.

I glanced around, getting the lay of the land. This was the perfect little setting for a two-bit drug deal. Hopefully, no one else would have that idea in the next few minutes. I created a tentative exit strategy, a quick get-out-and-get-gone plan for the event of things going sideways.

The alley was unlit, but as luck would have it, the moon was bright and unobstructed that night, sufficient for the pictures I needed to capture the moment.

Another twist. A commotion began to arise from the car, but not the kind I expected. It seemed an argument was in progress. I heard a loud slap—it looked as if Hicks was on the receiving end—and he climbed out, upset, and began walking in my direction.

As I heard him draw nearer, I remained as still as possible, though I could almost hear my heart pounding. Surely he hadn't spotted me. Had he?

The car fired up, pulled beside him, and Alyssa rolled down her window. "You're a liar!" she spat. "You lied to me!"

Hicks must have been figuring that he'd gotten more than he'd bargained for with this younger vixen. I wondered if he might be thinking of ditching Alyssa to meet someone else. It was obvious that anyone other than Alyssa was the better investment of his passion at this point. Who knew—maybe even his wife.

Regardless, he leaned in, took her face in both hands, and spoke, resuming whatever apology he'd been making earlier. Perhaps all the alcohol was keeping his temper in check.

Coolly lit by the moon, smoke rose from the car's muffler, and it created the frame for the scene that followed. Alyssa, her face caressed by the man she called a liar, leaned toward him for a kiss. Hicks's thumb blotted away a stray tear that gleamed on her cheek.

The kissing became more intense, and I knew makeup sex was in the offing. But at much closer quarters than I'd planned for. It was all going to happen right there, with the engine running and smoke billowing—a steamy love scene. Actually fairly cinematic.

He reached down to unbuckle his belt, but she pushed his hands away impatiently and took charge of the unbuckling herself. Soon the door swung open, and she was on her knees before him, doing what she felt would please him most, just minutes after calling him a liar.

The problem with filming something is that you have to watch what you're recording. I received no pleasure at all from watching him lean backward and forward, massaging her hair with his hands and speaking words of love as he urged her on.

When it was over, she attended to her makeup, actually looking around as if checking for an audience. I could almost detect disappointment that she didn't find one. Raising the stakes adds to the thrill sometimes and apparently, she was proud of the little adventure she'd just had. Something to liven up the diary, or perhaps water cooler conversation at work.

Next day, I figured a pretty severe hangover on his part was the cause of why he never left Alyssa's house. A car drove up, and a pizza boy leaped out to deliver dinner. Other than that, the door was sealed until Sunday morning. I know, because I was keeping watch—the problem with keeping watch is, you have to be there for it, though you don't get any pizza.

Through the night, I listened to the radio and disciplined my mind to keep alert. My eyes never left the front door. At any second, Hicks could emerge from it, and I had to be ready to be on the move when he was. I was rooting for that to happen, cutting short my stakeout, but in the end, I was there for fourteen hours, sipping on bottled water and rationing my granola bars. Empty bottles provided restroom facilities.

Meanwhile, I thought about those TV watchers and movie lovers who think people like me have a glamorous job. Nothing is what it seems.

Nonetheless, I was still gathering information that would prove useful, but I'd already accomplished the primary goal: enough damning evidence to show Mrs. Hicks, beyond any doubt, what her husband was up to behind her back. He had no path to denying his actions.

If she were to decide on divorce, she had powerful ammunition for alimony and adequate child support. In fact, *EXHIBIT A* would be my surveillance video—no alibis—no apologies.

· · · · · · · · · ● · · · · · · · · ·

"Well?" she asked over the phone.

"Let's meet and talk about it." I named an area café.

"But is he? I mean, is he having—"

"I think we need to talk about it face to face. Do you understand?"

"Okay." I heard the despair in her voice. She had a pretty good idea what she was about to hear. She had to hear it, and she was impatient to hear it, and she dreaded to hear it.

She dressed nicely, wore a light blue sweater and ensemble, but the truth was that she looked years older than she had at our first meeting, a few weeks ago. She smiled faintly as I stood to greet her, and we sat down together at the little table. I slid a large envelope across the table—the moment she knew was coming. It contained my report and my invoice, but also the things any spouse dreads to see: pictures and video evidence of marriage's cruelest betrayal; things that must be seen and can never be unseen.

I hadn't said a word, but my eyes met hers and saw the tears beginning to come. She continued to look at me and finally when she could find her voice, she said, "You caught him."

I nodded. I've found that it's best to say as little as possible in a meeting like this. Nothing I could say would be a salve for the pain. I can only hope my supportive presence, along with my available ear, provide some slight consolation for the moment. In those instants, I hate being the messenger bearing the photographic evidence, justice notwithstanding.

I got up from the table and said my only two words for the meeting: "I'm sorry."

As I began to walk away, Mrs. Hicks said, "Thank you for catching him. Thank you, Mr. Hopson. All you did was confirm what I already knew."

I nodded, pleased, I suppose, that she wasn't angry with me—that can happen—and I walked away with the flat emotions that always follow this kind of case. It's always good to move on to something new, and I never need to look back. No follow-up is necessary unless I'm called to testify in a deposition or in the courtroom. If I let myself get into a habit of checking in, I might grow emotionally attached to a case. As a good detective, I can't be a good friend.

But the Hicks case—that one didn't follow the usual rules.

Just as she had the night of the condo surveillance, Mrs. Hicks kept placing calls to me. She was worried about his emotional state. What could I do? I could at least listen. So I did.

Hicks, it seemed, had issues other than marital unfaithfulness. He was bipolar; he'd battled substance abuse issues for years. Mrs. Hicks said, "He's battling some pretty terrible demons, and I'm getting worried about what he might do."

A few weeks went by, lawyers got some arrangements in order, and Hicks was served with divorce papers, along with video evidence of his affair.

More time passed, the divorce was finalized, and Hicks began to unravel, from the inside out. He drove to his ex-wife's home to see their twin seven-year-old daughters one last time. He talked quietly with them and gave them stuffed teddy bears, with cards, candy, and a long, lingering hug. Never before had he held them so tightly.

They walked him to the car, one holding each hand as they looked up at him, and one of the twins said, "We miss you, Daddy." His eyes teared up, and then he found he couldn't control his weeping. His daughters watched the car disappear around the corner, sad that they might not see him for several more days.

"No limit," said the other little twin. She was reading the vanity plate on the back of his car. Perhaps they wished some things, such as visitations by daddies, really had no limits.

Mr. Hicks was renting a house in the area. He went there and sat down in a living room chair. The silence amplified the emptiness he was feeling, and he seemed to gaze into a sad future that gazed back at him… tears in his eyes reappeared.

He rose, looked through a linen closet, and found a small blanket. Returning to the chair, he wrapped the blanket around his head, then clicked the safety off the handgun in his lap. He held it to his temple, squeezed the trigger and found that finally, he could stop weeping.

It was Mrs. Hicks, whose worst fears had come true, who found his body the next day.

As I've said, I walk away from cases; I make a clean break. My clients don't stay on as friends. But that case has stayed with me. It haunts my thoughts at times, particularly late at night, and I suppose it always will. When I think of Hicks's age, thirty-nine, and the young age of his twin daughters, I can't escape feelings of personal guilt and complicity in an awful tragedy. Usually, I can feel that in some small way, I've helped people. I've made the world a better place.

Not this time.

You chased a cheater, and you caught him, I think. *It's on him, not you. Something of the kind would have happened sooner or later. You were just caught in the crossfire.*

I tell myself these things.

But who am I kidding?

CHAPTER 2
How Would I Know?

*"In theory, there is no difference between theory and practice.
In practice there is."*
Yogi Berra

All of us love the idea of a clean slate, a fresh start: "Today is the first day of the rest of your life." We want to think the past is just what the word implies, irrelevant history.

The old baseball pitcher Satchel Paige said, "Don't look back; something might be gaining on you." I think he's the one who has it right. We never entirely leave our past behind. We are the sum total of our experiences, our upbringing, and particularly the families that brought us into the world and set us on our feet.

If you had a loving and present mother and father, you enjoyed a terrific head start on life. If there were significant issues in your home, you weren't immune. You began your journey with a little extra baggage to carry. Not that this can't be overcome; many great achievers do so all the time. As the saying goes, I never met a strong person with an easy past. But let's not pretend our past has no significance.

Studies show that about ninety percent of brain development, intellect, social skills, and personality occur by the age of five. Whatever happens or doesn't happen in your family will play a role in that all-important stage of human development. Nobody chooses his or her family. But we do have an opportunity to take the good, identify and discard the unfortunate, and learn from the whole experience.

It doesn't always happen. Sadly, we know that children of alcoholics are more likely to repeat the miserable experience of their parents, and children of divorce may do the same. But this isn't destiny. We do have the opportunity to look our family history squarely in the eye and choose to live differently.

My father and mother divorced when I was six years of age. The demise of their marriage was justifiable to say the least... I stayed with my mother during those early years, and she worked hard to care for both of us. Each month she had to work hard to pay our rent for the tiny apartment we shared. Nonetheless, I was not capable of appreciating that kind of thing when I was so young. I was a headstrong kid who came to understand her sacrifice only with the benefit of time and hindsight. But she's still around to refresh my memory.

As I entered my adolescence, I was fortunate enough to get my bearings and avoid veering off-course in life, as some do. But my mother then married a man who made it clear he wanted no children—including existing ones. So, I moved in with my father who had a new wife, too; one who happened to live out of state.

I found myself in a new world of staunch work ethic and discipline. At that stage in my life, this wasn't a bad thing. I needed a strong role model who was willing to be fair but firm, and my dad filled those shoes. Even then, I understood that there was no perfect home, and I was noticing that my father wasn't always around in the evening. He'd stay out late, or even, on occasion, fail to come home at all. To my young mind, it was understandable. After retiring from law enforcement, he worked as a bounty hunter and also owned a bar in New Jersey. He wasn't going to live by banker's hours; bars were late-night establishments, and capturing fugitives, I knew, were often focused on things that happened under the street lamp. My new stepmother didn't share my ambivalence toward his absences, and I heard the arguments.

I was a teenager, and on those long Friday and Saturday nights, sometimes I sat with my stepmother and waited for my father to come home. The hours became progressively later, but I continued to mark it off to occupational hazards. I never put two and two together. Whatever the reasons for his tardiness, they were good reasons relating to his bar or his bounty hunting. But I watched my stepmother's face and saw her concern. I felt sorry for her—a spry, Greek woman who calmed her nerves by smoking through packages of cigarettes. Fresh pots of coffee probably didn't help her nerves, but they did keep her up, where she could make sure her man returned home in one piece.

One particular midnight, I watched her wait, sip from her coffee mug, then take a drag of the moment's cigarette, halfway down to the filter, and place it in the notch of the ashtray. She glanced in my direction as I got up, turned down the TV set's volume, and said, "He's not coming home tonight. He's..."

Something dark came across her face. "What do you mean? How do you know that, Justin?"

I had rehearsed the moment, but I hated every second of it. It's a cliché, but time really did seem to stop. She just stared for a second or two, processing my words, but then, for a short time, was relatively composed. I think she'd harbored suspicions of her own, and I wasn't telling her anything genuinely shocking—apart from the fact that I, his son, knew about it.

Still, saying it out loud changed things. Both of us felt the tension. I had made real the elephant in the room.

My stepmother lit another cigarette, sat back, and finally, the tears began to come. Oddly, I think she appreciated me at that moment. I was his son, but I had expressed a kind of concern for her, a sense of fairness. But life wouldn't be the same after this; I knew I was changing everything, but I was also taking the only action that would allow me to live with my conscience.

As a result of blowing the whistle on my father, he spit in my face one evening.

That same evening, he shoved the kitchen table into my chest and called me an asshole.

Struggling to maintain my composure, I wiped his saliva away and thought, "This is the end of it. Between him and me. He'll never trust me again." That made it real, and my eyes filled with tears.

The divorce between my father and stepmother followed in due course. It was then that *unhappily ever after* became my perception of marriage—and divorce, a new normal.

I knew how it felt. I saw how it felt to my stepmother. And I could begin to see the terrible, chaotic ripple effect it has on a family, on a community. Nothing is more sacred than a family bond, and nothing is more tragic than the needless shattering of that bond.

As for me, I wasn't really sixteen anymore. Not inside. I was too young to be old and too old to be young.

I haven't seen my father in many years. The consequences of his divorce(s) and our dysfunctional relationship have been long-lasting. Though invited, my dad neither attended my wedding nor has he ever spoken to his grandchildren and as I see it, those actions say it all.

It's an unfortunate situation. But if I had it to do over again, I'd do it again. My integrity is important to me.

· · · · · · · · · · ● · · · · · · · · · · ·

I did what I could to hide the deep emotions and sense of loss I felt and returned to the business of being an adolescent on the edge of adulthood. Life had to go on. I graduated from high school, and proceeded to college and then to grad school. Somehow, I still held onto my dream of going into law enforcement, even if I wasn't holding onto the one who inspired that dream.

Just a few days after terrorists hit the twin towers on September 11, 2001, I entered the New Jersey State Police Academy. The twenty-three-week, boot camp experience instilled a level of discipline and crisis management that far exceeded my expectations. Upon graduating, I received a badge, a gun, and the power to enforce the law.

NJ State Police Academy Graduation

As a trooper, I learned more than law enforcement; I learned a lot about people, their problems, and how to work with them. As I investigated the gamut of criminal activity, wrote traffic tickets, interviewed witnesses, interrogated suspects, investigated accidents, handled domestic violence incidents, and helped victims of crime, I was getting the best possible course in understanding basic humanity. I felt I had made the right career choice, and if I ever did anything else, I'd be better prepared no matter what my new direction might be.

Life seemed settled for me. What I didn't realize was that another intense defining moment lay in wait for me. It happened one ordinary day as a rookie trooper when I witnessed an example of police corruption that disturbed me. I'd been on the job for only eleven days.

Ethical dilemma. Everybody faces one sooner or later—the day you're confronted with a choice that tests you to the core of your beliefs.

We were engaged in a relatively routine traffic stop. My training officer arrested a woman for drunk driving. What could be the problem with that? The woman was not behind the wheel at the time, and the arresting officer knew it, I knew it—we all knew it.

The woman we arrested was in the backseat of the car. As I watched incredulously, my training officer arrested her anyway and falsified the report. Most people understand that when a driver violates the law somehow (such as driving drunk), only that driver is liable. There's no law against being an inebriated passenger.

Yet this was happening, and my name was on that false arrest report. I thought to myself, "I didn't sign up for this." So, I made it known I wouldn't testify in court in support of that arrest, and I also told the prosecutor it was an improper arrest. Among officers, that's drawing a line in the sand, and it's simply not supposed to happen. The "blue wall" of law enforcement officers is supposed to hold firm.

The charges were rightfully dismissed once the video of the unlawful arrest surfaced, but not the memory of what I'd done. I was labeled a whistle-blower, and it wasn't going to be tolerated—not for anyone who wore the badge, but *particularly* not for a kid who'd been on the job for eleven days.

I never planned on being a whistle-blower—I didn't plan for it as a father's son, nor as a state's trooper. What I did plan on, somewhere deep inside, was maintaining a clear conscience; living a life of integrity; sleeping well at night because I knew I'd honored my principles in all my decisions. When faced with situations that weren't simply questionable, but black-and-white wrong, I couldn't just "go along to get along." I wasn't wired to sell out.

Now, in the locker room, I felt the eyes of all the other officers on me. My life veered into a dangerous journey of hazing and harassment. This may sound like the script for an overly dramatic TV movie, but I was targeted by a secret society of state troopers known as the Lords of Discipline.

I was physically assaulted. My car was vandalized. Hate notes were posted on my work locker, and threats were both implicit and explicit in my work life. Troopers were caught running my license plate accessing my personal information…then the intimidating telephone calls in the middle of the night followed suit, seemingly to bully me into submission. I was ostracized by the law enforcement community, and finally, choosing my timing, I blew the whistle on the Lords of Discipline. This sparked the largest internal investigation in state police history and led to a high profile federal case. I've already told that story in great detail in my previous book (*Breaking the Blue Wall: One Man's War Against Police Corruption*).

There has been a time when I genuinely admired my father and aspired to follow his steps. Both my father and the career he chose brought certain levels of disillusionment. While we're products of our past, we're not chained to it. We have the opportunity to find out who we really are, rebound from our disappointments, and build something new. I'd like to think that's what I've done. I learned what truly mattered to me—the life of abiding by integrity, being a faithful husband, and loving father to my children.

By now, you have a better understanding of why I feel the way I do… why I've committed to honoring the truth, and why I am a sworn enemy of cheating in all its sordid varieties.

CHAPTER 3
Private Eye 101

*"The world is full of obvious things which nobody
by any chance ever observes."*
Sherlock Holmes

Anyone diligent enough to study can learn the skills required to be a detective. In fact, this book will be your blueprint on how to chase down and catch a cheater. But let's not get ahead of ourselves. You need to know a little of the history of this profession, too. To know where we're heading, we need to understand where we've come from.

The phrase *Private Eye* brings to mind any number of popular TV and movie characters. But it actually dates back to the 1800s and a detective named Allan Pinkerton. Born in Scotland, he's still considered America's first private detective. The Pinkerton National Detective Agency was hired to protect Abraham Lincoln and one of his top generals, George McClellan, during the Civil War.

Pinkerton went on to help chase down Wild West outlaws such as Jesse James and Butch Cassidy. His life was actually more colorful than the average TV detective inspired by his work. His agency lasted until 2003, when it was absorbed, along with the almost equally famous William J. Burns Detective Agency, into a network called Securitas Security Services USA.

But most of us don't think of large groups when we hear this term. We think of the private detective, the lone wolf played by James Garner (*Rockford Files*) or Tom Selleck (*Magnum P. I.*), the clichéd "straight shooter who plays by his own rules." There's something about this character that captures the American spirit of independence, toughness, and dogged pursuit.

Films like *Chinatown* and *The Maltese Falcon* have carried the private eye genre into movie theaters. And even today, new versions of Sherlock Holmes (for the British spin or American adaptation) and others show that the fascination with this work never ebbs. We even listen to sensationalized PI music: "Private Eyes" by Hall and Oates and my personal favorite—the Dire Straits' classic "Private Investigations."

We love private detectives—unless we need one, or find one on our own trail.

• • • • • • • • • ● • • • • • • • • •

The P. I., as everyone knows, wears soft shoes, suitable for creeping around quietly—thus, as early as 1860, we began calling him a "gumshoe." We also recognize all kinds of clever tactics he might use to get his information, but over the years, many of these have become archaic.

Like every other kind of work, a private investigation has been modernized and enhanced by new technology—particularly the accessibility of revealing databases, the availability of social media, as well as gadgets of the latest and greatest variety.

For example, GPS tracking devices are incredibly helpful. For you, Melania, it might not be possible for you to attach such a device to the famous Cadillac known to insiders as "The Beast," carrying the president through traffic. Security wouldn't allow it. But in more ordinary cases, as long as a car, motorcycle, airplane, or boat is titled in your name, and you have a financial interest, you can legally use a global positioning system (GPS) to track your mate's physical movements. Like the GPS you might have on your dashboard, it will pinpoint a driver's precise movements anywhere on Earth. I should note that different states have varying laws, so ask a lawyer about GPS regulations where you live.

Attaining evidence is the name of the game, and new tech offers every advantage. Consequently, most PI's relish the opportunity to hunt for clear and incriminating photographs—one "burst mode" at a time. It's the thrill of the hunt for evidence, which is the intriguing part of my line of work. But there's also the matter of outwitting a target who will be making some kind of effort at covering his or her tracks. The effective investigator outsmarts targets and documents the process clearly, which is no easy task unless a target is incredibly reckless.

Cleverness counts, then, but good interview skills do, too. Most of us believe we know how to carry on a discussion, but winning trust and guiding the conversation toward pertinent information is more of an art than a science. These often-informal chats will eventually be stitched into a strong narrative that will persuade the judge and jury in a courtroom.

As a matter of fact, a proficient PI does everything with the courtroom in mind. Unlike the badgering of some police interviews, the conversation of a wise investigator can be subtle and highly skilled, extracting credible info casually—and therefore more dependability. Trust and respect are key ingredients in dialogue.

A good interviewer will never need to interrogate. He'll forge a bond with the witness, empowering that witness to share an important story that delivers fruitful information.

The crucial difference is this: The PI carries no local or federal authority—merely the authority that comes with personal respect. The interviewee is under no obligation to talk at all, much less share a statement or affidavit. He or she may have every reason to "stay out of someone else's business." If the investigator makes the wrong approach, lots of slammed doors may result. And once that door slams, it's unlikely to open in the future. A potentially valuable witness would be lost.

One conversational misstep, one poorly placed sarcastic remark, one instance of unwanted pressure, and the inexperienced PI will learn a painful lesson. That's why, as much as investigators appreciate their gadgets and their technology, they know that two ears and a mouth are the most powerful tools they possess.

How should you start an interview?

Introduce yourself. Be friendly but professional. Disclose the law firm or company you're representing and briefly explain why you're there. That is, you're investigating this particular civil or criminal matter.

Even at this early stage, empower witnesses by giving them a sense of proud responsibility: "Listen, I could really use your help in finding something out." Or, "I understand you may have some information that would help us see that the right thing is done. You could make a big difference."

"Really? Me?"

Asking for help is a powerful bonding agent. Its fundamental human nature to say, "Sure, I'll help," if we make it very clear that we have a need they can fill. And by endowing that witness with a sense of importance and civic responsibility—or perhaps just the call to do the right thing—we honor that person. We form a bond; we even establish some basic level of teamwork: "Hey, you and me, we're working together on something important." If only for a brief chat.

Hopefully, you've got the witness's attention and interest. You've created the environment of cooperation. It helps if a witness is *intrigued*. And let's face it, when people are our business, every case is intriguing to some extent.

Intrigue is a bit like a sommelier—a wine steward—pouring a glass of fine champagne. He or she knows exactly how to make a small performance art out of the simple act. If you or I poured that glass, there would be nothing compelling about it at all. In the same way, a capable and experienced PI can tell you a neighbor's old tabby cat is missing, and instantly command your intense fascination.

The investigator should be genuine but gentle, interesting but not sensational, commanding without being manipulative or pushy. The worst-case scenario is for the witness to feel a sense of being cornered or pressured. The slam of the door will soon follow, and worse. After a round of phone calls, other doors might fail to open to you.

The two ears/one mouth principle holds true—the more you listen, and the less you talk, the better you'll do. The TV detective from central casting will say, "Yep...Yep...Mm-Hmm" while jotting things down in a notebook, but don't believe it. Better to listen attentively, maintain eye contact, and show just a hint of surprise when pertinent facts materialize. Write down basic stuff—dates, names, times, numbers—and never mind with the narrative for now. The story will fill itself in later.

As the conversation comes to a natural close, it's essential to express sincere appreciation: "You've really helped me. Thank you so much for this, and if I think of another question, may I call again? Let me know when the best time for that would be. Also, I'm going to leave you with my phone numbers, office and cell, as well as my email address. Hey, again—thanks!" Don't overdo it, but be affirming.

Would you have expected us to discuss posture? It's part of doing things the right way. Don't stand directly in front of witnesses, stare into their eyes, or do anything that might seem physically imposing. If you've rung a doorbell, you might take a step back once the door is opening. The body language says, "Relax—I'm not a threat."

You're not Detective Columbo. The frumpy and uncombed thing worked for him, but it's not a real-world thing. If you look presentable, people will be more likely to trust you. And as well as the tough-as-nails persona worked for Humphrey Bogart, you're better off killing 'em with kindness instead of cool detachment.

And yes, you need to be a student. That is a student of human behavior. If you're not a veteran people watcher, good at observing how and why people do what they do, you're going to struggle. Listen and see all that you can; talk and assume only when necessary.

I've never met someone with an innate understanding of human nature any more than I met a child born with a knowledge of algebra. It just doesn't happen. There's a learning curve, and it materializes while you're watching people and the subtleties of physical theater. You'll begin to pick up on gestures and signals you never noticed before and facial expressions that offer information as valuable as what comes through words. A silent witness may still tell a story, if not the kind you can use before a jury.

・・・・・・・・●・・・・・・・・・・

As I've mentioned, law enforcement officers and private investigators shouldn't be confused. PIs don't point guns at suspects. They don't put handcuffs on criminals. Law enforcement officers protect and serve on a federal, state, county, or municipal level.

Law enforcement is public service funded by taxpayers; private investigation is undercover service based on client contracts. Most PIs are hired by attorneys, insurance companies, businesses, or individual clients to investigate civil and criminal matters. And no matter how many TV mysteries you've solved, please be assured that PIs have no power to arrest.

And, of course, everyone's curious about guns. Process serving, cheater-chasing, and undercover surveillance carry potential dangers, but carrying a handgun only heightens liability. Personally, I choose to arm myself in the field. That's why I've obtained a concealed weapons permit and maintained proficiency with a handgun. In the unfortunate event that I need to use the weapon, I'll be able to do so safely, legally, and prudently. Still—the gift of gab is far more important to what I do.

Author and private investigator, *Justin Hopson*

I've mentioned some of the things PIs investigate. My career narrowed to a focus on divorce work. Sometimes there are benefits to specializing, and for better or for worse, divorce became my niche.

Not that I would take on all such cases. Before accepting one, I carefully consider what my investigation will involve. Am I going to focus on child neglect, substance abuse, infidelity—or all of the above? Have there been prior criminal issues? I have to look at the big picture before launching into a case for an attorney or an individual client.

Once I'm involved, my work will be to gather information for the client. But to get that far, I have to collect a good bit of information for myself, just to help me decide whether or not to go forward. Divorces, as we all know, are complicated and emotional and explosive. Someone like me needs to know what he's getting himself into.

All the same, when a client comes to me with warning signs, along with a suspicion of cheating, I find that more often than not, the client's intuition is accurate. If it's a maybe-and-maybe-not situation, my client may say, "Gee, I don't know. My spouse may be totally innocent, and then I'd feel so guilty about hiring you."

In that case, my advice is this. "Sir (or ma'am), It's good to know the truth. It's better to have the evidence and not need it than to need the evidence and not have it." It also makes a difference later, in a potential courtroom situation. The more tangible evidence one has to present, the stronger the case will be; the more it will help alimony or child support judgments; the more the truth, in general, will be brought to light. And that's nearly always a good thing for all parties involved.

I've mentioned that divorces are complicated and messy. Every situation comes down to "he said" and "she said." Solid evidence becomes crucial in getting beyond what anyone may claim. What happens in the absence of real evidence? The whole case is a crapshoot. The judge may merely split everything down the middle in civil court, or make a generic no-fault-type settlement, truly unfair to someone who has already suffered far too much, and something too much like a reward to the cheater.

• • • • • • • • • • ● • • • • • • • • • •

I'll answer the question most people are probably eager to ask.

How much does it cost?

The hourly cost for *licensed* private investigators varies from state to state. I've seen rates as low as $60 per hour and as high as $200 per hour, in different locales. There are other expenses to be taken into consideration, too: mileage, video editing fees, background checks, a fee for testifying, etcetera.

An initial retainer fee of $1,000 or more is typical, of course, and you'll receive a written contract documenting the fact. Read it, make sure you agree to it, and sign it before paying that retainer fee. It's good protection for you and the *licensed* private investigator for services rendered.

I mentioned that word *licensed* again. I'd like to reiterate the importance of hiring that type of investigator. These should be bonded, insured, and always provide a written contract prior to conducting the investigation. Each state has some extent of regulations and oversight that licensed private investigative businesses adhere to. In my home state, for example, the South Carolina Law Enforcement Division (SLED) regulates licensure for a private investigation business. Some of those regulations are three years of requisite investigative experience, a $10,000 surety bond, SLED approved contract, license fee, fingerprints, and comprehensive background screening.

Source: "New Private Investigative Business License" *SLED online;* Revised 7/2017; *http://www.sled.sc.gov/Documents/PI/pilicnew.pdf*

What about an unlicensed PI? Perhaps you came across one and found out he or she would save you some money. As in everything else in life, it doesn't pay to cut corners that are there for a good reason—and particularly with private investigators. Cheap, in this case, may turn out to be expensive. There are plenty of fly-by-night "investigators," amateur sleuths, wannabe cops, and fringe agencies who will not only fail to serve you—they'll make a bad situation much, much worse. Use your own imagination concerning what could happen with a botched surveillance, as well as how it would be regarded by judge and jury.

Consequently, a private investigator should be licensed, bonded, and insured—that is, if you want the right information provided in the right way, leading to the proper settlement.

CHAPTER 4
Love Thy Neighbor

*"If you take someone back after they cheated,
they'll think it's okay to do it again."*
Unknown

EXHIBIT B is an investigation that unfolded in the Carolinas circa 2015:

If I had to do it over again, I'd trust my intuition on the Lippincott case. It was a case that shook my faith in marriage. In fact, for me, it marked the beginning of the end for my pursuit of cheaters as a private eye.

It started when I was talking to a good friend over the phone. We'd known each other for years and trusted each other implicitly. We spoke of many things: kids, the aches, and pains of aging, neighborhood goings-on. Then Heather Lippincott's name came up—just a casual mention. An uncomfortable pause ensued. I didn't really want to say much about this subject.

"I've seen Heather getting a little too close to a local tennis pro," I finally said.

"Seriously? Marcus Lippincott's wife?"

"Afraid so. Their interaction at the tennis club. Their time together outside of the club—it doesn't pass the sniff test. She's getting emotionally and maybe even physically attached to a guy with a history of womanizing."

My friend took this in and then said, "Well, I probably should tell you what I know. Just remember you didn't hear it from me, okay? You're on the money. Drew has been chasing Heather for a while now."

Drew, of course, was the tennis pro.

He continued, "I don't think it's physical, but I agree—there's no doubt something's up."

"Four kids," I said. "She has four kids and a husband who worships the ground she walks on. I think she and Marcus were even high school sweethearts."

We chatted for another minute or two before my friend had to get off the line. He said, "Hey if anyone can get to the bottom of that, it's you."

A week or two passed, and I kept my eye on the tennis pro every time I was at the club. Heather and Drew worked out together, something that seems made for flirting. I thought about Heather's husband, putting in long hours to support her lifestyle, while she cavorted with this guy.

In full view of everyone, Drew would place his hands on her hips and legs, supposedly demonstrating the game of tennis. Clearly, every move had a secondary meaning. Heather wasn't the only one captivated—the rest of the club was buzzing about the inevitable. Had it happened yet? How much longer before they were an item? What did Marcus know?

Some of Marcus's friends knew all about it, but they weren't telling him. If they had, surely the curtain would have come down on this little sideshow.

Marcus was known as a successful businessman and a loving husband, but he wasn't keeping up with current events. Heather was one of those desperate housewives with a little spending money, a club membership, and too much time on her hands. It can be a recipe for a poisoned marriage.

Heather was leading two lives, one socially respectable and the one publicly scorned.

Suppose someone approached you romantically, telling you they were married and living with a fifth spouse and had seven children by four different partners? I'm going to guess you'd run in the opposite direction. That was Drew's relational résumé, but somehow, Heather didn't find it disqualifying.

One other thing: Drew was eighteen years older than Heather.

At this point, you might assume this guy must have been ruggedly handsome. Not so much; other than having perfectly coiffed hair, his looks were ordinary at best.

These situations don't run on any ordinary human logic.

· · · · · · · · ● · · · · · · · · ·

Being wired (and trained) the way I am, one day I followed Heather from the tennis club to a local restaurant. Just as I anticipated, Drew pulled up a chair at her table, and they ordered lunch together. This was a date, and it was hard to imagine either of them coming up with an innocent cover story should the need arise.

I had no camera; I wasn't on this case in an official capacity, and frankly, it was none of my business. I was there as a friend of Marcus Lippincott, as someone needed to be. I believed he deserved to have one friend who was watching his back and would tell him the truth.

I wouldn't enjoy doing that, but I'd had to bear such a message on any number of other occasions. Lots of bad things can happen when you open those curtains, and I did know how to avoid at least some of the dangers. So, this was something I needed to do.

First, I needed to do some homework. I looked into Drew's situation in a cursory way, and the plot thickened immediately—Drew had more than one iron in the fire. And this time it was right in my neighborhood.

Near me lived a woman of Asian descent who, it turned out, was another of Drew's current conquests. She and her husband had been married for eleven years. They had a reputation as a devoutly religious and upstanding couple. And notably, their two children attended school with the Lippincott kids.

It would seem that Drew wrecked only the finest homes. And as far as all the kids knowing each other, it apparently thrilled Drew to creep right up to the edge of exposure. This wasn't a love triangle but that deeper betrayal, a love *square*. I've found that many of these things if they happened in a movie, would seem "unrealistic." But as we know, fact is stranger than fiction.

Another private eye was already covering this second affair, and he was the one who brought me up to speed. Drew was good for the detective business, I suppose, but I was doing this on my own time. It was a matter of simple right and wrong, close to home.

I laid it all out before my wife, asking what I should do. She listened carefully then said, "Go for it." She was accustomed to my being waist-deep in the dirty laundry of others. She rolled her eyes at the idea of a "love square." Geometric adultery.

"One issue to think about," she said. "If you do uncover what Drew does, you'll uncover what you do as well."

My wife was right. Unless they were very close friends of ours, most neighbors had no idea what I did for a living.

I could still be an investigator—just not of the "private" variety.

•••••••••●••••••••••

That was a Monday. On Friday evening, I was ordering takeout at a local pub, and who should I see there but Marcus Lippincott?

He spotted me immediately and offered a friendly wave. I felt the uncomfortable prod of my conscience. *Say something, Hopson—if not you, who? If not now, when?*

I put on the best smile I could find and walked over to his table. "How's it going, Justin?" He asked. "I'm all alone."

"So I see."

"Yeah. Heather's out with a few friends tonight, and all four kids are at a birthday party. I'm on my way to pick them up, soon as I grab a bite to eat."

"You know that I have two kids of my own," I said. "They grow like weeds. Before we know it, they'll be babysitting us."

He smiled at the joke and said, "Hope I live that long."

A waiter informed me my takeout order was now ready. I pulled out a credit card and said, "Would you put my friend Marcus's dinner on that card as well?"

Marcus didn't see that coming. "Wait, what?"

This was the moment. I placed a hand on his shoulder as the waiter walked away. I looked Marcus in the eye and said, as gently as possible, "No easy way to tell you this, but your wife—she's not out with her friends tonight."

For a second, he sat with his mouth open, as if he'd taken a sharp blow to the gut. Then he found the words to say, "What are you talking about? My wife—"

"No one wants to tell you this, Marcus. She's having an affair." My grip firmed on his shoulder, letting him know I was on his side.

He had that awful look in his eyes, the initial moment of disbelief, and he was shaking his head *no*. He wasn't ready to accept the unacceptable.

"His name is Drew," I said. "Local tennis pro at the club. They've been together for a month or so. I'm sorry, Marcus. I thought you should know."

I reached for my wallet again, this time producing a business card. "I'm here to help," I said.

He roughly pulled his shoulder away from my hand. "I don't believe what the hell you're saying! Get the hell away from me."

Those are always words to take seriously. I signed my receipt, grabbed my food, and gave Marcus one more glance. His demeanor was somewhere between tending to his pain and throwing a punch. Or maybe asking me a question. Instead, he stared a laser burn into the table.

I knew I'd planted a seed—painful but necessary.

• • • • • • • • ● • • • • • • • • •

Heather was missing in action at the club for a few weeks. Drew, on the other hand, had no choice but to be there. He was definitely off his game; his swagger having taken leave.

Perhaps for the sake of appearance, she did return to her lessons, and inquiring eyes watched as they attended to their tennis with much more caution and formality. People figured the little courtside scandal had run its course, but they were wrong.

As time went by, and they sensed the coast was clear, the lovebirds fell back into old patterns. Flirting, giggling, a bit too "hands-on" for the situation. I had to wonder what Marcus was thinking—how could he allow his wife to come within the same zip code as the guy he'd known was in the picture romantically? Could he be that naïve, or was he that non-confrontational? Or did he just not care?

One Sunday morning my phone rang. I saw I had four missed calls and a text: "Please call ASAP." It was from Marcus Lippincott.

I tapped out a reply, but before I could hit send, some flare of intuition stopped my finger. I sat, stared at the phone, began spinning and flipping it in my hand, and realized this was my trademark nervous tic. Only a matter of time before my wife noticed and pointed it out.

I was thinking about me. I had to live in this neighborhood. I had to see these people at the gym, neighborhood pool and even at church—the Lippincott's were fellow congregants. Shouldn't I let sleeping dogs lie, even if they were sleeping on the wrong mats?

My conscience replied, *Love thy neighbor.* Its voice is quiet but carries a great deal of authority.

Still, I waited until Marcus called again. His tone had lost the anger. "Hey, can I come over to your house and talk? I need your help."

I took a deep breath—*Here I go*—and said, "Where can we meet?"

"Anywhere you'd like to ride. I'm in front of your house," he said. A look out the window confirmed that Marcus had pulled up in my driveway.

"What's going on?" my wife asked, joining me at the window.

"Hornet's nest—I'm about to stick my hand right in," I said.

She sighed, knowing I had to do what I had to do.

I checked out Marcus's face as I climbed into the car. I'd seen that one before—the empty gaze, gray pallor, unhinged jaw. He was in the midst of coming to terms with a truth that would undermine his life and his cherished values. The love of his life was cheating on him. There could be no emotional equilibrium after such a revelation.

For me, there's no greater sin, no crueler act of cold treachery than marital infidelity. You stand before an officiant, before the world and make a solemn vow, only to break it, along with breaking the lives of your betrothed, your children, and all those who care about you. And for what? A few minutes of pleasure here and there?

This kind of moment is about listening, and that's what I did for hours on end, nodding my head occasionally, offering a word to show I was hearing him. Toward the end of his long, sad story, Marcus asked, "How much do you charge and when can you start?"

"Let's talk about a plan first." I mapped out a route to catch the philandering couple, advised my friend what to expect, and let him know about the financial requirements. He agreed, and within hours, Heather Lippincott's SUV was being tracked by a GPS device. I was also able to document more than seven hundred text messages between the wife and Drew.

An associate of mine checked social media, printing out all the cryptic messages and pictures between the two of them. We found this was a regular, quite careless element of their affair. Dancing near the cliff's edge.

I ran a comprehensive background investigation on Drew and became his shadow every time he left the house.

It took six days to gather enough photographic and video evidence to prove motive and opportunity. There was another development, too: Drew's own wife received an anonymous package—chock-full of damning photographs, when she found out what was happening, threw him out of the house, and filed for yet another in Drew's string of divorces.

It was basically a slam dunk, all hard evidence, and Mr. Lippincott was in a position to be granted a fault-based divorce from Heather. Case closed. Or so I thought.

The next day, I happened to walk into the locker room of the club, and there was Drew, changing clothes. He looked up, saw me, and glanced away quickly. "You weasel," I said, under my breath. But I wasn't going to leave it at that. I walked up to him and said, "Drew, your habit of dating married women is a dangerous one. Over the years, I've seen guys like you maimed by angry husbands."

He just sat unclothed and contemplated.

"Let me ask you something," I continued. "Why do you do it?"

"I don't. I don't—go after them. They come after me. You might not believe it, but it's true."

My gaze flickered just an instant toward the guilty body part before I reclaimed eye contact. "Interesting. You're either the most misunderstood person I know, or my suspicions are correct. Either way, you're on notice. You're being watched. Might want to start thinking with the head on your shoulders instead of the one between your legs."

•••••••••●•••••••••

Marcus was another matter. Even with solid proof in his hands, he managed to retreat to a state of denial. "She said nothing happened," he insisted. "Drew was pursuing her—she admitted that—but she swears they're just friends. Nothing more." He shrugged.

"Marcus. What about the seven *hundred* text messages? Three-hour visits to his condo? Restaurant dates? All the photos and lies we documented? All due respect, but you're tangled up in a web of deception."

Like the other guy, he had trouble making eye contact. "We're going to counseling," he said. "We're working through everything. That's all I can tell you."

What more could I say? "Fair enough. I'm just giving you the benefit of my personal and professional experience. When someone cheats on you and you take them back, the odds are in favor of more cheating in the future. Counseling is great for a lot of issues in marriage, but cheating is a different animal."

Why wasn't I surprised when Marcus called again? It was a few weeks later and another SOS distress signal. But the lost, confused tone was now replaced by a trace of fury. He'd been duped, and he knew it.

By this time, his marital calamity was a matter of public record. The neighborhood, the club, the local church—everyone was clued in. Nosy neighbors had their own local reality show to talk about, including my role in exposing it. My wife had been right—this one had hit a little too close to home.

Appropriately, we met at the same pub where I'd first broke the unwanted news. Three guys I knew from the neighborhood were sitting at the bar. I discreetly claimed a stool on the other side, waiting for Marcus, but the other guys walked over and wanted to buy me a beer. Good ol' Southern boys, wearing shades with Croakies, pastel shorts fastened by whale belts, the local drawl. I smiled and declined their beer, thanking them for the offer.

"What—no drinking on the job?"

"Not exactly," I said, vaguely.

"Hey, I hear you're a modern-day Sherlock Holmes. That true?"

Another chimed in, "Not spying on any of us, are ya?"

All in good fun for them, but it rubbed me the wrong way. I let the chuckles subside, then stood, looked at each of them square in the eye, paused one beat, and said, "Good night."

Out on the pavement, I sent my wife a text: "You were right."

Exposing you might mean exposing me. No good deed goes unpunished.

I connected with Marcus, and we rerouted our meeting. When we got together, the first thing he said was, "She pulled the wool over my eyes. I blame her more than I blame him—and I'm filing for divorce."

Anyone who has ever done that understands the painful truth: Filing?

That's the easy part. A single flick of a wrist, sign on the line. What follows is lengthy and grueling and leaves a mark on the soul that nothing can scrub away. There are damaged emotions, the unending financial drain, the loss of your good name, and worst of all, the deep and desperate pain of your children.

Love is the greatest of all treasures, and on the other side of the fine line is the most profound of miseries. Such a thin wall between heaven and hell. Not an enjoyable place to build a career.

I told Marcus, "You might consider teaching this tennis pro a lesson on Guy Code. Namely, not sleeping with another man's wife."

Marcus asked, "And I would do that how?"

"Eye for an eye," I said.

Marcus blinked a couple of times, as he took in the implications of my words. I watched his fists clench, probably unconsciously, and he said, "Could you bail me out?"

"Not a problem."

The next day, Marcus indeed aimed for the eye when he came across Drew. The punch was a good one, leaving a laceration the size of a dime, just beneath the eye. It had to hurt.

Drew took a knee—clearly a lover, not a fighter—rubbed his wound, saw the blood, and looked at his attacker in disbelief.

Marcus, ready to land another blow, said, "Are you done?"

"Yes," said Drew. "I'm done."

Ten stitches would mend the wound. His ego would require healing that only time could provide. His problem was apparently much more elusive, because a few weeks later, Drew and Heather were at it again, with the divorce still being hammered out. Once it was final, she became his sixth wife. You've heard the one about tigers changing stripes. I'm here to testify that some lessons simply can't or won't be learned by some people.

Last time I saw Drew, he was at the tennis club, newly married, with four new stepchildren in tow. Anyone could see these "unintended consequences" were adding a bit more responsibility to his daily routine.

I smiled, hopefully with obvious irony, and said, "The new normal?" He nodded, too weary to contest the issue. I sat down, did the math, and computed that among Drew's stable of six wives, he was on the financial hook for eleven children scattered across three states.

CHAPTER 5
You Do the Math

*"Statistics are like bikinis. What they reveal is suggestive,
but what they conceal is vital."*
Aaron Levenstein

I'll lay my cards on the table: When it comes marital infidelity, I place little stock in statistics.

As a matter of fact, the more you know about any one subject, the more you're likely to notice how frequently the numbers fail to tell the whole story. Example: Presidential polls. Stats have their roles to play, as long as we take them with a very healthy grain of salt. No matter how well-planned a poll is, or how careful a research study may be, there will be a blind spot or two—i.e., *Trump vs. Clinton polling in 2016*.

What I've seen, up close and personal is the breakdown of marriages in my community. So, I know the numbers don't quite capture what's out there.

Why? First of all, "numbers" are dependent, in this case, upon the very human individuals who provide them. Most of us are highly subjective—more apt to be emotional than rational—about our relationships. We may not choose to give an honest answer, but even if we do, sometimes we're fooling ourselves. Too many folks out there tell themselves they have the perfect marriage, built to last forever, right up to the moment when it implodes. And when it comes to answering questions about faithfulness, "cheaters gonna cheat" that is, they'll be unfaithful to the questionnaire by lying.

Secondly, infidelity statistics are questionable without the inclusion of gay marriage. This, of course, has been legalized in the United States, and the LGBT community (lesbian, gay, bisexual, transgender) must be factored into all empirical research concerning divorce and infidelity. Statistics otherwise are incomplete.

In writing this book, I considered the official statistics. But for the most part, I drew the conclusions I've reached about cheating and the deception behind it from my own personal experience. Also, I've drawn from many interactions and interviews with adulterers, marriage counselors, pastors, psychiatrists, marriage counselors, and of course, spouses who have been betrayed as well as those who betrayed them.

• • • • • • • • • ● • • • • • • • • • • •

Throughout history, adultery has been seen as everything from a crime to a personal sin to a very bad idea. Even today, in some Muslim societies, it's punishable by stoning.

Even apart from the strict enforcement of religion, adultery is most often the sin most often whispered about, a lapse too serious, too immoral, and certainly too personal to discuss in public. But it's not uncommon and never has been. I would suggest that every red-blooded American alive today has felt the effects of it in some way. You might have cheated or been the victim of cheating. You might have comforted a friend, family member, or co-worker whose life has been disrupted by adultery. It might have invaded your own home when you were a child, helpless in watching your parents go from loving nurturers to combatants.

No wonder we watch so many television series like *The Good Wife* romanticizing cheating spouses and reality shows such as *The Bachelor* glamorizing a man's lack of monogamy. Americans have also grown accustomed to reading about extramarital affairs in tabloids and in the mainstream media. As I pen these pages, Donald Trump and his alleged sexual misdeeds are on a national 24/7 news cycle. The question we fail to ask is, how much do these items of pop culture normalize a sinful act to be kept at arm's length? Is there really a line in the sand that society won't cross? How desensitized are we? It can be made to look glamorous, even righteous in some twisted way, by the right script and production values.

Think about successful movies such as *Indecent Proposal, American Beauty, Closer, The Intern, Unfaithful, The Other Woman,* and many others.

Sometimes, in a film like the notorious *Fatal Attraction*, cheating is shown in a negative enough light. It seems like a thrill ride at first, just like in real life—only to veer out of control into tragedy. Not that anyone expects the partner they cheat with to turn out to be a knife-wielding psychotic. In the end, most depictions of cheating are glamorized. They're shown in soft focus, and by their very frequency, seem to be something just about everybody does.

This book takes a very different, very un-Hollywood view. My goal is to stand in traffic, holding a "no trespass" sign to potential cheaters, and an "emergency detour" sign to those who have been cheated upon. Having seen the effects of adultery, I believe it's the kiss of death to marriage and monogamous relationships. If it can be avoided, there's the chance of a wonderful life together, crossing into the autumn years with the kind of shared contentment that only long-term marriages can enjoy. If it isn't avoided—and all it takes is one bad day, one weak moment—the road of opportunity for that long-term contentment narrows to the point of being almost impassable. In boxing, a knock-down blow may not mark the end of the fight. Maybe the boxer staggers to his feet and fights on. But usually, the contest is over.

Cheating is a knock-down blow, and it's tough for any relationship to survive it. Cheat and marriage is "down for the count."

Some readers will be uncomfortable with my pessimism about the hope of reconciliation. Aren't all things possible if we set our minds to it? Whatever happened to forgive and forget? Pastors and people of faith quickly point out that marriage is an ancient and divine covenant, that all civilization is built on marriage and the family as a permanent, unbreakable foundation stone, no matter what human failures darken it. They point to the book of Genesis and God's commissioning of Adam and Eve.

In response, and with equal reverence for biblical truth, I point to Matthew 19:9, in which Jesus declares, "And I tell you this, whoever divorces his wife and marries someone else commits adultery—unless his wife has been unfaithful." Those final six words imply that God is just as negative about adultery as he is positive about marriage, for Jesus leaves an out for those who have been cheated upon. In other words, divorce can be a mercy wide enough to cover the terrible victimization of cheating.

God tells, us, "I hate divorce," in Malachi 2:16, but he adds, "So be on your guard, and do not be unfaithful." A reasonable reading of these passages is that as much as God despises the death of a marriage through divorce, he despises, even more, the cruel act of adultery that precedes it. He is a God of law and justice, but also one of comfort and mercy. It's good religion, but it's also good common sense.

I've been asked by pastors and therapists alike, "What do you consider cheating?" Good question and my answer may surprise you.

I define cheating as an *emotional or physical* connection with someone outside one's marriage or relationship. We think of adultery as a physical act, but the real issue is the connection and the commitment required by marriage. Cheating can occur long before I take a picture or a video of it. It could even happen over the Internet or smartphone before two cheaters are in the same physical location. That's a kind of epidemic these days, by the way. Some websites and apps exist for the sole purpose of helping husbands and wives cheat, and while statistics are even more inadequate in something so virtual, studies have shown that Internet cheating is widespread. More about that in the next chapter.

It's really not about the physical act—necessarily. When a married person opens up to anyone other than a spouse those channels of the heart that we think of as romance, cheating has occurred. There's such a thing as an "adulterous heart." A solemn vow has been made, possibly considered sacred and before God. Two people have pledged absolute fidelity to each other. Once either partner veers even slightly off course, we have to realize this is no small moment, either for that individual or his or her marriage. For example:

> *"A striking paradox is that while polls such as Gallup indicate 90 percent disapproved of extramarital relationships, a national survey reported that 15 percent of wives and 25 percent of husbands had experienced extramarital intercourse. When emotional affairs or sexual intimacies without intercourse are included, the incidence increases by 20 percent."* Source: American Association for Marriage and Family Therapy.

This statistic gives us a picture of men, women, and their affairs in the USA. It's alarming to see the disconnection when you consider 90 percent of them disapprove of infidelity—their actions suggest otherwise. More alarming, perhaps, is what I call the Two-Thirds Theory. I believe that without a significant social shift away from infidelity in America, sixty-six percent of marriages and monogamous relationships in America will face online relationships, affairs of the heart, and/or casual sex outside of marriage in the near future. The trend is away from faithfulness, not toward it. But once again, am I too pessimistic? Infidelity in two out of three relationships?

Yes, I'm on record saying that without a cultural *sea change* towards monogamy, 66% of marriages and monogamous relationships will experience cheating.

My theory factors in the LGBT community and Millennials. Millennials make up 25 percent of the United States population. This generation was born between the years of 1980 and 1999. Millennials are more socially connected by technology than any prior generation. Their tech-savvy allows for social media, dating apps, pornography, online dating websites, and chat rooms at their fingertips 24/7, as well as rapidly brewing emotional relationships with multiple people, simply by a tap or a swipe on a tiny screen. Not to mention, the temptations of futuristic relationships with AI (Artificial Intelligence) looming. In their lives, connection by technology is all Millennials have known…so there's an ease to keeping tabs on their ex's social media page and frequently liking the social media posts of someone they find attractive and texting a coworker coquettish memes & messages; e.g. "micro-cheating." Though I don't believe micro-cheating is cheating, I do believe it's a breach of trust, intentionally flirtatious, and can lead to a physical or emotional connection with someone outside of one's marriage or relationship. In America, it's the new normal.

On the other hand, isn't it true that divorce rates have been dropping? A couple of decades ago, after a famous magazine story, everyone was buzzing about a 50 percent divorce rate—a controversial and disputed figure. Again, statistics may not lie, but they tell confusing stories.

As Millennials show ambivalence toward marriage, we can expect to see a resulting plateau in divorce rates. But we have to consider divorce rates in tandem with marriage rates.

Sam Sturgeon, president of the research group Demographic Intelligence, told The Boston Globe that he projects the marriage rate will fall to the historically low level of 6.7 per 1,000 people, which includes those getting married a second and third time.

Statistics also suggest that America is becoming more secularly progressive and less religious. The two items are connected. If a wedding is seen as a religious ritual, a godly vow, and God begins to fade from the cultural picture, we can expect marriage to seem less essential. According to the Pew Research Center, the quantity of Americans who describe themselves as Christian has fallen from 78 percent to 71 percent, while the number of atheists, agnostics, or those of no faith has risen from 16 percent to 23 percent.

The largest growing group of all is known as the "nones"—that latter, no-faith category. Followers of religious trends have dubbed this era a "Post-Christian" or at least "Post-Christendom" one. That is, Christianity, while far from dead, is no longer seen as the guiding influence of Western culture.

Religious culture in decline has a natural connection to traditional marriage in decline. But adultery never goes out of style. Marriage and the nuclear family may no longer be the universal pattern, but adultery rates continue to climb.

You might think, as I did, that the USA is the world's most adulterous nation. Remarkably, that's not true—nor is this country on the Top Ten list in that category, according to Statista Internet portal for statistics. Thailand, for some reason, sets the global pace. Well, more than half of Thai survey respondents admit to adulterous affairs. We can only wonder if what the survey really measures is honesty. In any case, Thailand is followed by a lineup of nine European nations, Denmark and Germany being the most affair-ridden.

France, coming in at number five, is an example of the cultural impact of infidelity. The reputation among travelers is a beautiful country with a rude populace. Or is it rebellious? Half of the French seem to believe that having an affair is morally unacceptable, while in America, nine out of ten frowns on infidelity.

・・・・・・・・●・・・・・・・・・・

Now that gay marriage has been legalized, the question becomes what effect this will have on infidelity. Will the LGBT community embrace monogamy? Will gay men, lesbians, and transgendered individuals be more, less, or equally monogamous in comparison to heterosexuals? How will the LGBT community impact the trend of infidelity and divorce rates in America? Time will tell.

Once more, we take statistics along with our observations. Either way, it's an open question how the changes of the present—the entrance of Millennials and the acceptance of gay marriage—will affect the future of American infidelity. Both segments have the capacity to create a cultural revolution of monogamy.

Yet I remain skeptical that any cultural force in current view is likely to reduce the growth of extramarital affairs. Some have gone so far as to tell me that monogamy is unnatural or unrealistic in these times. In an age of science, we're told that our species is one more branch of the animal kingdom, in which less than five percent of mammals are monogamous. Men, it is said, are primitively wired to be sexually pluralistic. Historically—even among certain biblical heroes—polygamy has been a constant trend. But the most common argument of the twenty-first century is that we as human creatures are no more than the sum of our physiological impulses. If we're genetically predisposed to continue seeking new mates, they argue, why worry about it? Cheating just represents the new stage in human enlightenment.

All these arguments can sound persuasive. Science has a certain built-in credibility that works the same way as statistics—it says, "Would I lie to you?"

Yet science doesn't cover all the depths of human feeling and experience. Statistics don't capture who we are and how we see ourselves. History marches on, we tell ourselves we're more enlightened, and we wander away from our religions and our honored traditions—but a pesky impulse continues to prod us from within. Some call it the conscience.

We still have a hunch we should let our conscience be our guide, and what it says is this:

> *There is right, and there is wrong. You know the difference, and you've always known it, without being told. The act of marriage, the moment of bonding in a wedding, feels like something on the side of right. Cheating on your partner, the betrayal of vows, the treachery against your spouse, and all the effects that go with it—all of that feels like it's on the other side. The one we call wrong.*

Maybe you don't believe in conscience. Maybe you believe right and wrong are superficial human constructs, convenient or inconvenient, rules made to be broken. Even then, simple common sense should tell you that if monogamy isn't for you, if you don't believe in bonding for life—*don't get married!* Live in harmony with convictions or lack thereof. Whatever you may miss in terms of the joy or the pain of married life, you'll certainly bring less pain and suffering to yourself and others by making, then breaking, what the Bible calls a union of "one flesh."

If you do choose to pledge a vow to the "honorable institution" of marriage, and to one special individual—live in harmony with *those* convictions. Discipline yourself. Work to make your marriage the best it can be, growing ever closer in your union, and protecting yourself from temptations to be unfaithful.

And if you can't decide what you think about this marriage thing—consider moving to France!

CHAPTER 6
Lovesick to Lost Love

Isn't what we mean by "falling in love" a kind of sickness and craziness, an illusion, a blindness to what the loved person is really like?
Sigmund Freud

"If I can't have him, no one will!" It sounds like something from *Fatal Attraction*, but these are words heard in real life.

Dr. Ana Maria Gonzalez-Angulo, a breast cancer doctor, was having an affair with her colleague, Dr. George Blumenschein. The two of them worked together in a cancer facility in Houston, Texas. They were close associates, experts in dealing with the deadly disease, so they spent much time together. She had begun sitting on his lap as they conferred over some issue, and then one day she turned and kissed him. From there, the relationship grew physical.

But it never really took off—not to the level of the full-blown relationship Dr. Gonzalez-Angulo wanted. Dr. Blumenschein felt that what he saw as a brief period of flirtation had run its course. He rejected the other doctor and turned his attention back to his live-in girlfriend of ten years, with whom he had decided he was ready to start a family; the extracurricular activity was over.

The more he rejected Dr. Gonzalez-Angulo, however, the more obsessed she became. "No does not mean no to her," he testified later.

Finally, when it became evident that the word meant exactly that, she invited him to a light breakfast where she had "special coffee from Colombia," which she laced with ethylene glycol, a sweet-tasting chemical found in antifreeze. Later, he felt "tipsy" and found he couldn't stand up.

Dr. Gonzalez-Angulo hovered close to him the rest of the day, including helping him eat his dinner when he could no longer lift his utensils or even his phone.

The next thing he knew, Dr. Blumenschein found he was lying in a hospital bed. Now fighting for his life, he couldn't be sure who had passed him the poison. But he had a pretty good idea—and the object of his suspicion was right there in the same building, where she worked. What if she returned to finish the job?

He also wondered if his girlfriend, Evette Toney, was safe. Making an accusation was risky, but Dr. Gonzalez-Angulo was arrested, and later convicted. According to KRPC Houston, she was sent to prison for ten years.

Dr. Blumenschein survived the attack, but with kidney function reduced to forty percent. He was left to wonder what in the world got into his colleague? How could someone who had taken the Hippocratic Oath, including "Do no harm," have staged such an attack on someone she said she loved?

Is there such a thing as love gone toxic?

• • • • • • • • • ● • • • • • • • • •

My college years were like those of most other people. I majored in a field (Psychology), sowed a few wild oats, and did a whole lot of coursework I didn't even know I was doing—that is, the greatest education colleges and universities may teach: people skills.

It's been observed that the teenage years make us the center of our own little universe. It's a confusing time when we try to work out who we are, why our bodies are changing, and where we belong in terms of a close-knit group of other teens.

But the years that follow, at the next level of education or in the workplace, are devoted to our place in a larger universe. We meet a greater variety of people. We get our first, introductory studies in the busy world of society. There are no grades for this course—ultimately, it's pass or fail.

I attended a diverse university and also held down a night job as a bartender, and I can't imagine a better perch for the observation of people. Where is there a better opportunity to listen? Where will one hear more confessions of who people are, as their inhibitions melt away by the glass? On a typical night, I would interact with scores of faces new to me, and I'd hear about every conceivable hope or dream or fear.

The barhop's job is to pour the drinks. He never shows that your story has grown tiresome, giving you the brushoff. He must hone the discipline of pure, unconditional listening. But when those monologues do seem to ramble, when they wander in circles, he can do something valuable: search for motives; question the influences that brought on this state of mind. And if he's spending his days listening to psychology lectures, he's even more likely to take this cue.

If he begins to group people in specific categories—those bored with life, those repressing their resentment of bad bosses—he would quickly establish one of the world's greatest motivators of barroom despair: "She did him wrong." Or change the "she" to "he." Any bartender will tell you that lovesickness is great for the alcohol industry.

I have yet to meet anyone who hasn't seen several good examples of what it means to be "truly, madly, deeply" in love. A great many people haven't just seen it—they've lived it. And they know there's no crazier roller coaster ride than the topsy-turvy trip of being sky-high with love, then plunging into deep despair when that love fails.

As a matter of fact, it's a spectacle so familiar, so age-old, that we take it for granted. It's the subject of a hundred thousand favorite songs and date night movies. Why take it seriously? Because to anyone who's been through it, it's serious business. And because it can derail someone's life in the same way any other addictive influence can. More and more, psychologists are coming to grips with lovesickness as a genuine pathology, even in some cases a disorder with physical and chemical components.

But it needs a more serious name than lovesickness. One of the terms that have come to the surface is *limerence*.

• • • • • • • • ● • • • • • • • • •

Dorothy Tennov was a psychology professor several decades ago. She wondered why science was so interested in a vast panorama of human behaviors, but never showed much interest in the craziness of romantic love. She wanted to know whether it was all a myth of pop culture, or if it was a universal human experience that ranged from every culture.

She researched thousands of personal accounts of lovesick people—not people who'd merely found a compatible partner, but those who felt intense, obsessive love. And indeed, she found a pattern that cut across languages and cultures.

You might have learned that certain chemicals are released in your brain at certain times. We now understand a lot more about this than in the past. As you can imagine, when we're sexually attracted to someone, or we feel aroused, chemical activity is intense. Dopamine is one of the primary chemicals that is released. This word is taken from *dopa* plus *amine*. Dopa (or "dope" for short) is the amino acid that gives us a mild sense of excitement—a high.

Dopamine pathways in the brain are connected to *reward-motivated* behavior—a good feeling. Cocaine, for example, releases dopamine. When we talk about a "rush," that is, a sudden, almost giddy feeling, such as a gambler experiences with a winning hand, or a football fan when a touchdown is scored, we're often talking about dopamine release. When we find something that makes us feel good, of course, we seek more of it.

But there's another chemical called serotonin. It's an integral part of us that is a kind of emotional "checks and balances" system. It restrains and regulates strong emotion. Let's say you're sitting in church, and someone quietly sits next to you and whispers very good news in your ear. Your team won a huge game. You want to say, "Yes!" and pump your fist. But serotonin kicks in and says, "Not here! This is a church!"

Here's what's important. In an intense dopamine rush, serotonin *decreases*. Again, relating to a football game, this is why, if you're a huge fan, you'll jump up and down and hug a stranger in the stadium. Restraint systems are down. Serotonin is off duty. Dopamine is taking control.

Why do we "fall" in love, instead of merely meeting someone nice and deciding to commit to a relationship with them? Because it's a substantial dopamine experience. The human being has a strong drive to bond and reproduce and survive as a species, so our bodies reward us for finding a particularly appropriate partner. Serotonin steps out for a while and lets you go a little wild. For a particular time, fewer actions are out of bounds.

A female client comes to me and says, "Why is my husband acting this way? He's gone crazy! He used to be so restrained, so careful about things, and suddenly he'll walk into a restaurant with this woman, right in public, where any of our friends might see him. Or even me!"

She'll think about it a little more and say, "He went out and bought this new speedboat. He's wanted one for years, but we couldn't come close to affording it. We still can't. But he went out and bought it anyway—in his new, expensive clothing. And since when is he into piercings? Where did my real husband go?"

He hasn't gone anywhere; he's just "hooked on a feeling," as the old song says: "I'm hooked on a feeling, and I'm high on believing that I'm in love with you." He might believe this is a higher level of existence, an almost spiritual thing—which is why people write love poetry, compose songs, etc., and search for new expressions of their love. But what's happening, scientists tell us, is more like a chemistry experiment.

No, that doesn't sound very romantic, but for many people it's true. He gets a pleasurable amino acid release in his brain whenever he thinks of, pursues, or interacts with this person. "I've never felt like this," he says. But he probably has—it was just that the other times, he was a kid on Christmas morning, or a guy on a fishing trip catching the big one, or it was the time he got hired for that job he wanted.

Being crazy in love, however, is a process that keeps offering new dopamine rushes, and the extended time element can do a whole lot of damage. He may be dulled to the reality of it now, but he won't be forever—science tells us that, too.

• • • • • • • • • ● • • • • • • • • • • •

Being truly, madly, deeply in love feels like forever, but in reality, studies tell us it's an eighteen-month experience, more or less. It might be twelve months, or it might, at the most, be twenty-four. That's plenty of time to find the right person, get married, even start a family—which is the overarching purpose of the whole event, given our membership in the human race.

The only problem is that limerence is no respecter of marital boundaries. Married people fall head-over-heels in love with someone else just as unmarried people do. We don't *necessarily* stop falling in love just because we've gotten married—not if we don't regulate our emotions and keep a cool head. Married people feel attractions to others, but typically, the serotonin says, "I'll take this. You're married now, so settle down." And the dopamine rush is quenched and shown the door, more or less. It's a matter of human discipline, morality—call it what you will.

I've already written my feelings about statistics. You can well imagine "statistics" about love, such a subjective thing, may not be overly trustworthy. So, different studies have different results on how often we fall in love. According to one study, four times in a lifetime is about average. But all the studies agree that it doesn't stop just because we've found a mate. In the one-in-four study, almost one in five respondents claimed they met the love of their life *after* getting married to someone else.

In the next section, I'll offer some of the traits of the limerence experience, but first, I'd like to go ahead and detail the scariest part—the end game. As you can imagine, limerence intensifies until it seems to burn itself out. No matter what, it will come to the end of the wick. If it didn't, our world would be filled with crazy people who never got anything done, never left the side of the people they were so passionate about. In the ideal situation, we fall madly in love while single, and we marry—though not everyone who marries does so after a limerence experience; some are less susceptible, and the whole thing is fairly calm and orderly.

But married people fall in love, such as in some of the stories I've told, after building their families. They seem to go crazy, not caring what anyone else thinks, or what the repercussions may be.

Perhaps her marriage ends. She goes with the guy she's had an affair with, but the clock is ticking. At some point, she wakes up, comes to her senses, and says, "What have I done? Was that even me?"

I've seen it over and over. This is why it's so important that we understand what's really happening. Falling "head over heels" is a rush—until your head hits the ground.

IF THE FIRST LADY HIRED ME...

Here is what the specialists have helped us learn about the "lovesick" experience:

1. The object of our passion becomes irrationally wonderful in our eyes. No one else can compare to this "wonderful" human being. By the way, limerence can only happen with one object at a time. It leaves no room for anything or anyone else.
2. We accentuate the positive and eliminate the negative. If they write us a letter, we save it and read it over and over. We cherish pictures of them, and it's no use for anyone else to point out the bad side of that person. We won't hear it.
3. Life is a crazy ride during this period, filled with intense emotion, energy rushes, lost energy, sleeplessness, and losing interest in eating. Everything is turned up to 11.
4. Setbacks in the relationship, such as when the other says, "We shouldn't be doing this," just make us love them even more. Challenges intensify the adventure, just like in the movies.
5. Intrusive thinking occurs. That is, we can't think of anything else. Like everything else about limerence, there's a song for that: "You were always on my mind," Willie Nelson sang.
6. We become possessive, jealous, and terrified of rejection—all the usual responses of someone hooked on something. No one better get in the way. Crimes of passion occur when a truly jealous person feels that relationship threatened.
7. We will do anything, make any sacrifice for this person. We long to hear about something they want or need, so we can throw ourselves into finding it for them.
8. We're eager to make lots of changes. Lovesick people go on diets (especially since they lose interest in eating) to please the other person. They change their hairstyle, their clothing, even their car because they're always thinking about what might win favor with the other person.
9. Sexual desire becomes intense, and the thought of that person having sex with someone else is unbearable.
10. 10. But it's really not about sex. Oddly enough, people experiencing limerence think of it in more spiritual or emotional terms. They

long for a kind of "one flesh" union with the person they love. It's a holistic feeling of desire, and sex is simply the most intense way to express it.

11. It feels bigger than we are. Others may say, "Stop this," and we'll say, "I can't!" There's no off button, or at least that's how it feels. It's a force of nature—in a literal sense.
12. It passes like a massive storm, taking effect on everything in its path, then subsiding into a quiet aftermath, and we're left to survey the damage.

• • • • • • • • • ● • • • • • • • • • • •

Limerence has factored into several love triangles that I've investigated over the years. So many situations that end up needing my services are cases of obsession and forbidden love, and that's where limerence is often found. My job is made a little easier by the risky behavior people indulge in. Those who are chasing a chemical high are less likely to take precautions. If you didn't know different, you would think some cheaters want to be caught, but in reality, they're being controlled by an obsession that is in the midst of causing a lot of pain.

Glenn Close's character in *Fatal Attraction* is an example of what we might call limerence on steroids. It was a thriller, made purely for entertainment. But real-life cases of fatal attractions are not rare: two cancer doctors in Houston? It really happened. Some of these incidents make the news; most don't. But each obsessive love triangle has one point in common: a scorned lover. "If I can't have him/her—no one will!"

Most of us fall headlong in love at some point. Hopefully, it will happen at the right time and with the right object of affection. Sometimes our love is reciprocated; sometimes it's not, and we're heartbroken. Sometimes it happens when one party or the other is married, and things worse than broken hearts could ensue—divorce; possibly violence.

• • • • • • • • • ● • • • • • • • • • • •

Allow me to shift focus once again to *EXHIBIT D*—my investigation into the systemic violence, systemic cheating, and the murder of James Belli. Full disclosure, what you're about to read is the most tragic case that I've

IF THE FIRST LADY HIRED ME…

investigated…one that made news headlines for years…one not for the faint of heart:

Occasionally some cases come along, and I realize just how vast this world's problems can be. In the world of unfaithful marriage, I deal with relationships and individuals who have lost their way. But it's also worth recognizing there are institutional problems out there, too—deep problems far more significant than any one individual or family.

James Belli helped me to realize that. James was never married, never cheated, was never cheated upon—but as far as I'm concerned, a divorce cheated him of love and a system cheated him of life. And for that reason, I felt his story was worth sharing.

Lieber Correctional Institution is known as one of the most violent of maximum security prisons. Attacks on both inmates and guards are more than common. The situation has been so grave at times that officer positions couldn't be filled, discipline couldn't be upheld, and prisoners found they didn't have to respect the men guarding them. Take, for example, a 2015 attack on one officer in which he was stabbed with a broken broomstick, soaked with his own pepper spray, and savagely beaten for eight minutes before another officer turned up to open the cell door for him.

Nonetheless, I was called upon to investigate the circumstances surrounding an inmate who was attacked: 19-year-old James Belli. When the guards found him, he was clutching his throat, trying to stem the flow of blood seeping through his fingers and pooling around his body, where he lay on the hard floor.

He tried to say the words "Room 39," but it was no longer possible for him to speak clearly. His throat was severely cut, and he'd lost a lot of blood. His rescuers knew they were only allowing him a few more hours of life at best. After that, he was indeed pronounced dead.

Some people hear about the death of convicted criminals and say, "Well, good riddance to bad rubbish. Better that guy than some productive member of society." But sometimes it pays to look at the stories of those who made a wrong turn somewhere and ended up living—and dying—in a nightmare.

I was destined to learn a little of that story. James Belli's mother, Diane DiLorenzo, hired an attorney, and that attorney filed a lawsuit against the South Carolina Department of Corrections four years after his death. Ms. DiLorenzo needed closure. In particular, she wanted accountability for those who were complicit in her son's death. If some shred of positive prison reform could come out of it, if Lieber could even become something approaching acceptable, then she'd be able to move on with her life.

It was my job to find any evidence of corruption at the facility and developing any potential witnesses for the case against the state. This was a bit of a larger scale for me than, say, finding out if a husband or wife was cheating. I was dealing with an entire prison. But it turned out to be a defining moment in my career.

Due diligence alone was enormous. I had to study a copious amount of testimony, public records, and court documents to gain an understanding of the prison's standard operating procedures. Then, on the other end, I needed to learn all I could about James Belli, a man I'd never met. According to Ms. DiLorenzo, a divorce and the absence of a father played a large part in James Belli's juvenile delinquency. Ms. DiLorenzo told me that she and James' father separated when James was just two years old… shortly after that his father moved out of state. As a result of the divorce and feeling abandoned by his father, James began to seek attention in all the wrong places—drugs, alcohol, and thievery filled the void. In an attempt to straighten him out, Diane turned her teenaged son into police to face burglary and larceny charges. After a few mistakes and mishaps, James became inmate #00314458 at Lieber Correctional Institution.

What was a day in his life like? What about his killer? I interviewed every witness I could, and slowly I began to piece together, the best I could, the events leading to James Belli's death. I worked closely with David Savage, Diane DiLorenzo's attorney, and together we gathered sworn statements, prison records, and wire transfer statements. We lined up former Lieber corrections officers who were willing to testify on our behalf.

The picture that came together confirmed everything I'd heard about Lieber Correctional Institution. It's home to the state's worst offenders, and to make matters more dangerous; it's mismanaged and understaffed. That meant that an outlier like Belli, a nonviolent teenager (not yet twenty), suffering from bipolar disorder, could be labeled an escapee by mistake. Then he could be dropped into the middle of the worst, most violent sections of the prison—full of murderers, rapists, and the like. Again, a nightmare.

This prison had a grand total of two correctional officers on duty in James Belli's cellblock, meaning they were responsible for two hundred of the most high-risk inmates.

There was more evidence of mismanagement. The prison had failed to address the growth of violent gangs in the prison, along with extortion and drug trafficking. James Belli, we found, was easy prey for the more aggressive inmates. He was bullied, beaten, and threatened—pressured to be a conduit for transferring money in the canteen accounts of other inmates. He relayed his problems to his mother, who wired hundreds of dollars into the accounts of various inmates, in the desperate hope of protecting her son. But eventually, she ran out of money.

So where were the authorities? How could these things be allowed to happen in an American institution of the twenty-first century? Belli complained to them. He pleaded with those running the prison to transfer him out of the hell-hole where they'd dropped him. Every request was denied. His file said "escapee," even though he wasn't one.

One former correctional officer, now able to speak freely, told us, "I personally delivered at least seven transfer requests from Belli to supervisors, but nothing was done." He described how Belli wasn't particularly tall or strong, not compared to those in his cellblock. "James was so small compared to everyone else, that (other inmates) called him Little Jay."

Later, this officer signed a sworn statement giving his experienced opinion that Belli didn't belong in the violent setting where he was confined. As I left the interview, I thought, "This guy never had a chance."

And I had to know how he got there in the first place.

・・・・・・・●・・・・・・・・・

In 2018, a dozen years after his murder, I reached out to James Belli's mother, Diane DiLorenzo. Since that tragic day, she had to find ways to move on with her life, including moving out of the state whose prison system cost her a son. But she gave me her blessing on the idea of sharing

James' story so that his memory might do some good. She answered my questions, though so many answers remain elusive.

I also talked to David Savage, her attorney. He's an astute, straight-laced personal injury lawyer with whom I'd worked a few times over the years. Whereas a mother could tell me about her son's early life, the attorney could give me more facts about the case. I also read every public record available concerning James Belli. But no matter how hard I worked, the big picture never entirely came together. The puzzle was just missing too many key pieces.

Every new answer raised a new question, such as—Sure, he ended up in that cellblock because of the mistake on his file. But still, shouldn't something else have happened in this part of the process, or that one, to get it straightened out? What about the money transfers? What about the requests he made? I've dealt with institutional ineptness many times, just like most people. But it defied belief that at some time, at some point in this nightmarish scenario, *someone* wouldn't have given James Belli the break he deserved. Of all my many cases, this is perhaps the most chilling, the most confounding—particularly since news accounts continue to bring horror stories of guards being assaulted with broken broomsticks, entering the facility as good men and emerging with post-traumatic stress disorder.

Here's what I know. James Belli had a tougher adolescence than most kids. He was the product of a broken home. He had a drug habit—cocaine and marijuana—and he fell into a life of low-level crime, mostly burglarizing cars to support his addiction. Bipolar disorder certainly didn't help his efforts to move into adulthood with the odds of success on his side.

He had a mean streak by some accounts. He was no doubt a petty criminal, but not someone likely to end up on anyone's "ten most wanted" list. I look at his life and see any number of people I've met or known about. My conclusion is, his chances of getting his life together were very good. He had a solid woman, his mom, in his corner. If he could have gotten through Lieber alive, he had every shot at moving forward positively.

IF THE FIRST LADY HIRED ME...

Mrs. DiLorenzo couldn't help but think back to the day she called the police and turned in her son. It was tempting for her to blame herself for all that followed, but how could she have ever known? She'd discovered there were active warrants for James's arrest, and it was the right thing to do. He needed to face the music, and it would be good for him.

As it turned out, he was sentenced to eight years in prison for burglary and larceny. Then the bad breaks began to pile up. He found himself in the absolutely wrong place at the absolutely wrong time, and the predators came out.

A few months into his sentence, he was beaten viciously by another inmate. The next day, the same inmate returned, grabbed him, and held on tight while Jaquan "Sticks" Ferrell plunged a dagger into Belli's neck. The shank had been hand-crafted there in the prison.

Jaquan Ferrell was serving a thirty-year sentence for murder, assault, and battery with intent to kill, along with three counts of armed robbery. In such company, it's amazing Belli made it even as long as he did.

When the guards found his body, they couldn't make out his words at first: "Room 39." But a steady trail of dripped blood led to that very location. "Sticks" Ferrell and the inmate who restrained the victim were both housed there. This was an investigation that took no more than a few minutes. The murderer wasn't much of a master criminal, but his work was thorough and devastating. Jaquan Ferrell was sentenced to life without parole for the murder of James Belli.

The civil lawsuit brought by Ms. DiLorenzo against the South Carolina Department of Corrections came to a settlement of $450,000, allowing the state to deny any wrongdoing. A little money changed hands, but it's hard not to include that the most important changes failed to materialize. The prison's problems continue. Just as all of us deserve a faithful marriage or relationship, we deserve to have our trust in local, state, and federal government honored. If we try to cheat the government, we go to jail. But what happens when we're the ones who have been betrayed?

I believe James Belli was cheated of life itself, and his mother was cheated of the son who was precious to her—a lost love. Belli had his personal demons. Whatever root causes pushed him into a position where such a fatally disastrous course was possible, we'll never really know. I can only hope that somewhere, on the other side of this confusing life, Belli's soul is at peace, and he watches over the mother who tried so hard to watch over him.

CHAPTER 7
United States of ~~America~~ Entertainment

> *"Never allow someone to be your priority while
> allowing yourself to be their option."*
> Mark Twain

During the last century or so, what have been the most significant change agents for dating and romantic relationships? Urbanization, of course, as more people have moved to cities and drawn from a greater pool of possible mates; the invention of the automobile would be another.

One of the greatest of all would surely be the advent of online and mobile dating. How can romance ever be the same? Nearly everyone has seen an eHarmony.com commercial and thought, "Wow! You can do that? You can find the Mr. Right or Mrs. Right through a computer screen?"

Dating apps, virtual relationships, social media, and online matchmaking have been game-changers. Think about the shyer, less aggressive young man or woman, averse to the idea of walking into a bar, gym, or grocery store and trying to strike up a conversation with the opposite sex. Think of the small-town citizen who knows every single individual for fifteen square miles, and is pretty sure none of them are good matches. Think of the countless single men and women who have thrown up their hands and said, "Where am I supposed to meet anyone new?"

No wonder technology has revolutionized this perennial problem even more than most others. Match.com, Zoosk, OkCupid, PlentyOfFish and a growing number of other sites have become all but the default method of supposedly painless shopping for love. The Wall Street Journal and IBISWorld tell us that online dating has become a billion-dollar industry. An industry positioned for high-growth and upside in the United States of Entertainment.

One of the greatest appeals of this possibility is pure speed. We can all agree that we live in an instant gratification society, and a site that offers "plenty of fish" has the promise of offering variety and processing your relationship requirements quickly. There's also the cost factor. People are willing to sign up for a fee after they consider the cost of going out to meet someone, then going on several dates just to gradually discover if two people have enough in common.

And of course, online sites offer a research-and-logic based approach. You offer a picture and an informational profile, and they'll crunch the numbers and preferences. If you like to read and to eat Italian food, you're likely to find someone with the same preferences. If you don't like smokers, that factor will be ruled out quickly. If a partner needs to be Catholic or Baptist, again, consider it done. And it can all be dialed up on a smartphone!

Of course, some of the same old rules apply—such as being attractive and presentable. But there's an online advantage here, too. You can use a slightly outdated but flattering photograph. You can pad your profile the same way you'd pad a résumé on a job search. Most applicants apply a great deal of energy, time, and creativity to presenting an online representation.

For singles, it's a bonanza. For married people, it's a minefield. Consider again the small-town guy who found his wife—either locally or through a site—and has settled down in his one-stoplight community. But a bit of time has gone by, and married life isn't all that he thought it would be. Or perhaps familiarity has bred contempt. For whatever reason, he's restless. But if he cheats, everyone in town will know. Then he sees an ad for a dating site . . .

The market, of course, quickly responded to this kind of "need"—new solutions for the age-old desire for discrete cheating. In 2015, there was a data breach at the Ashley Madison website. It's become commonplace for even the largest sites, such as Yahoo, to be hacked and have information stolen. What made the Ashley Madison case different was that the site specialized in extramarital affairs. "Life is short," ran the tagline. "Have an affair." Fifty million users of that one site intended to do so. Thirty million users were exposed, and there was a whirlwind of divorces, lawsuits, and blood-in-the-water public shaming. One of the outed users, a professor at a Christian seminary, committed suicide after his name was made public in the data breach. Careers and marriages alike were ruined.

SeekingArrangement.com was even more focused on its market target. This was a highly successful site for "Sugar Babies" in search of "Sugar Daddies." In other words, a young and willing college student, willing to provide certain favors, could get a college education paid for by an older suitor. The typical Sugar Daddy, according to SeekingArrangement.com's CEO Brandon Wade, is fortysomething, earns in excess of $250,000, and is in search of a much younger woman. The University of Texas was listed, in 2014, as the site's top college for Sugar Babies. Legalized prostitution? You be the judge.

As any thinking person knows, most such temptations are too good to be true. All kinds of risks are entailed in using these sites—hacking, as embarrassed Ashley Madison users will tell you, being among them. AdultFriendFinder.com had its data stolen in 2016. This self-described "World's Largest Sex and Swinger Community" now had 400 million user accounts made public—while, of course, the entire appeal of such a site was its assurance of absolute privacy. Largescale selection can also mean largescale exposure.

· · · · · · · · · · ● · · · · · · · · · · ·

In my opinion, the most important risk factor is that of personal safety. The first case in point occurred on April 8, 2016, when Ingrid Lyne was brutally murdered. The single mother of three was the victim of a man she had met through an online dating service.

Ingrid lived in Seattle, where she was devoted to her three children and her patients; she was a forty-year-old nurse. But she wanted to find a soulmate. So, like millions of other Americans, she uploaded a photograph and information about her relationship status and interests.

John Charlton, 37, was a drifter with an extensive criminal record—the kind of thing that gets left off dating profiles, of course. He logged onto the same dating site and connected with Ingrid, whose picture he found attractive and whose location was convenient. Communicating through the site, they hit it off. Soon they planned a date at a Seattle Mariners baseball game.

They had basic information about each other. They had shared a bit of conversation. But what did Ingrid really know about John Charlton? Few users consider a particular factor of online sites: the lack of mutual friends to vouch for a potential partner. A common friend, for example, might have said, "You need to know that John has been spent time in jail."

Most of us, of course, are dreamers to some extent. When it comes to love and romance, we want badly to believe in princes on white horses and happily ever after.

The last thing we expect is to find ourselves on a date with a sociopath. Charlton couldn't approach his own parents, both of whom had filed an order of protection against him in 2006. He had been convicted of misdemeanor assault, misdemeanor battery, and felony theft. Would she have accepted the date if she'd read these relevant facts on his profile? If he'd uploaded his mug shot instead of a glamour shot? If she'd known he'd been incarcerated in two different states?

Here's what she did know, in John's words: "My intention is simply to make friends and meet up for a good conversation . . . not much of the crowded bar or club type. Mellow and quiet is more my scene."

Another problem about these profiles: No fact-checking.

• • • • • • • • • ● • • • • • • • • • •

When Ingrid's dead body—incomplete, but including head, arm, and foot—was found in a recycling bin, Seattle police followed the trail of forensic evidence to John Charlton and quickly linked him through the dating site. It wasn't a complicated case. When police looked in on Charlton, they found he had abrasions on his forehead, scratches on his chest and left hand, and an injured lip at the time he was arrested.

Homicide detectives later found bits of flesh and blood in Ingrid's bathtub drain, along with a fifteen-inch pruning saw. He was arrested, charged with first-degree murder, and later pled guilty to premeditated murder in the first-degree. Charlton was sentenced to more than 27 years in prison, which was the stiffest penalty under the state's sentencing guidelines.

The second case in point involves a newly popular term: catfishing. This is defined as luring someone into a relationship through a false online identity. Sadly enough, it has become incredibly common.

A 25-year-old Lashawn Johnson used a fake identity to meet 24-year-old Angela Russo online, by using false information about himself. The two of them made a date, at which time Johnson took the woman to his apartment for sex. There he trapped her in the kitchen and attacked her violently, eventually murdering her. According to the police, Johnson climbed into her car, drove it forty-five miles into the Arizona desert, set it on fire, and closed the matter—or so he hoped—by burying the body in a shallow grave.

What he didn't count on were the stories told by Angela Russo's cellphone records and Johnson's own live-in girlfriend, who was willing to give evidence. Claudia Martinez, an employee of the Arizona Department of Corrections, led detectives to the burial place and the site of the charred automobile, both of which her boyfriend had told her about the day after the killing. He had called her to pick him up not far from the place where he'd buried the victim, and he'd confessed to having sex with the woman on the night of her disappearance.

It wasn't as if the killer could take flight and elude capture. Detectives found him waiting for them in jail, for failing to appear in court on an assault charge.

Johnson confirmed that he'd made contact with Ms. Russo, as well as that she'd been at his apartment on the date of the murder. Further, he said that yes, he'd been in the desert area where her body happened to be found. In short, there wasn't much point in denying the obvious. He'd "made a mistake," and now his "life was over," he said. He wrote a letter of apology to Ms. Russo's family, asking for forgiveness.

Yet another woman came into the story. Brittney Johnson claimed to be Lashawn Johnson's wife—not to be confused with his live-in girlfriend or Internet date, whom he had murdered. Her story was that while Johnson had cheated, he hadn't killed Angela. The sheriff's office saw things differently, charging the suspect with first-degree murder, disposing of a dead body, sexual assault, kidnapping, robbery, and arson.

Angela Russo's mother told reporters, "Angela just went out on a date and ended up never coming home." Further, she warns the public to beware of the dangers of Internet dating.

• • • • • • • • ● • • • • • • • • •

Exhibit C is case #H11-073: Amber was a single, white female who sought my services. She made a strong and positive first impression. She had an Ivy League education and seemed to have it all together—a promising career in pharmaceutical sales, a sharp mind, and an attractive appearance. That appearance was on display online in the dating service she was using. It wasn't surprising she would attract a lot of attention and interest among the site's users.

Amber was frequently traveling to various cities for work, and she tended to be busy even when in town. So dating apps and websites made sense for her lifestyle. She was one of those people who hated the bar scene and felt that she didn't do well in crowds. "The casual aspect of mobile dating fits my lifestyle, and it's entertaining," she said. "I can meet someone in any given city and strike up a conversation. If all goes well, we'll meet."

I nodded and asked, "Entertaining, huh? So how may I help you?"

"Well—I might have found Mr. Right. Know what I mean? He seems perfect! On the other hand, I only know him online, so it's hard not to be suspicious."

"Mr. Right could be doing wrong," I said. "I can help you find that out. Before that happens, you need to tell me everything."

Amber did just that, and she spared no details. She told me about "sexting," lust, and virtual intimacy with a man who just might not be what he seemed to be.

"I thought we had something. But he lied to me," she said.

Amber seemed to think it surprising that anyone would lie online. I assumed everyone understood the Internet was a Liar's paradise, but I suppose some are a bit too trusting, or simply naïve. Mr. Right, she said, went by the name of Vincent. She pulled out her phone, opened the app, and showed me Vincent's profile picture. He wouldn't have been out of place in a men's fashion pictorial—green eyes, finely-chiseled jawline, jet black hair. "Sharp looking guy," I commented.

"Yeah—right? But he *lied*—about his relationship status."

Relationship status, of course, is the simple identification of whether someone is single, married, and/or divorced. On a dating site, it's the baseline from which everything else begins.

Amber was attracted to Vincent from the beginning, and she shared intimate photos and messages. The chemistry seemed to be strong, trust was established, and soon they were talking about meeting. Vincent was eager for the face-to-face and talked it up for weeks, but Amber's schedule was the problem. She just didn't have the flexibility. But they continued to interact over the Internet, as well as talking on the phone and via Facetime. Pictures were sent back and forth.

Eventually, the meeting took place, and both parties seemed excited, presenting their best selves. But now that they'd both shown up, the chemistry hadn't. Amber had imagined it would feel as if they'd been together for decades—a comfortable, intimate fit. "The physical connection was right there," said Amber. "But everything else was awkward silences and shallow conversation. It was so disappointing." Their time together came to an end, and they shared a kiss.

Despite the letdown, a second and then a third date followed. On this date, a few glasses of wine and a few words of love loosened inhibitions enough for an evening of casual sex. And after that, as they lay in each other's arms, Amber summoned the courage to ask Vincent about his past.

"Vincent, how long were you married," she said.

He stroked her hair, brushed her ear with his lips, and whispered, "It's complicated."

"What does that mean?"

Vincent took a deep breath, sat up, and began to explain how he was in the midst of a separation. There was a court struggle for custody of a two-year-old child, and it made the divorce battle even more intense.

Amber tried to take in what she was hearing. "Your profile—it said you're single," she pointed out.

"Well, really I am, that's the way I look at it. We're separated. I'm done with her, absolutely done with her. The divorce thing is just paperwork. In my mind, I've divorced already. But listen, this is our time together, right now. You and me. This isn't the time or place—I need you to trust me, honey."

A new day came, and Amber picked up the phone to call Vince. But she couldn't reach him. No matter how many messages she left, he wouldn't call back or return a text. Days turned into weeks, and Amber had to worry if her man had moved on—if her insistence on honesty had been a deal-breaker, and he was on the hunt once more.

Now she was coming to me. "I need your help," she said. "I want answers about who this man really is."

I told her I'd do what I could, but she was back before I could make much progress. Three days later, she was back in my office, a deeper level of frustration showing clearly. "Amber, could I see your iPhone?" I asked.

She handed it to me, and I began scrolling through her pictures of Vince. Something in one of those pictures caught my eye. In the shot, he had his left arm around Amber's shoulder. I transferred the image to my computer, cropped a small section, and enlarged the picture. Below the knuckle of Vincent's left-hand ring finger, the shade was two tones of color.

"Wedding ring tan line," I said. "Always hard to hide."

Amber's eyes were glued to the screen, and I wondered why she hadn't seen it—even looked for it—on their first date. The marking fades after a while, but when it stands out, as it did here, it hasn't been long since the ring was on. I pointed out the lack of hair and smoother skin on Vince's ring finger as compared to the rest of his hand.

Then I opened a folder, pulled out a printed sheet, and slid it across the desk to Amber. It was a social media post written by a Michelle, who was Vince's wife.

She was fifteen weeks pregnant. An ultrasound photo illustrated her happy words. And this was a brand-new post. I began to read the comments on the post as Amber grew angrier.

Stacy commented: "Soooo excited for Y'all!!!"
Mike: "Will it be a brother or sister for Vince Jr?"
Ronnie: "Due Date?"
Michelle: "June 2"
Catherine: "Congrats!!!!"

Amber now understood the ugly truth in full. She had been conned into an affair with a married man—given her heart, shared the deepest intimacy, on the basis of lies. In her mind, she had been careful and had eventually trusted Vince based on what she felt was her good judgment.

Now the question was what to do about it.

It was another one of those times for me to listen rather than speaking. Amber leaned back in her chair, closed her eyes, and finally said, "How could his wife *possibly* have failed to know he was cheating on her? He's living a double life! If he did this with me—he'd do it again, won't he?"

"That's how it seems to work."

"Maybe I should write Michelle a note or call and tell her everything."

The pain and hurt were deep. She leaned forward now and stared at the floor. I gently asked, "You gonna be okay?"

She shrugged, shook her head; she didn't know whether she'd be okay or not. I reached for a pen and jotted down the expectant couple's home address and phone number, and placed it in her hands.

Amber read it and looked up, startled—as if I'd read her mind.

"Some people are a mile wide and an inch deep, Amber," I said. "Vincent might need a rude awakening. More important than that—I'm sure Michelle would appreciate knowing the full extent of their relationship."

Case closed.

• • • • • • • • • ● • • • • • • • • • • •

In the old Greek myth, Pandora opened her box, and all the troubles of the world escaped. Online dating is a new, tech-savvy version of that box. It takes a sad song and makes it sadder. I'm left with a number of questions about this latest, "greatest" trend:

- What protective and preventive measures are in place to thwart criminals from using mobile dating as a predatory tool?
- Do online dating sites verify marriage records or sexual offender registries?
- Are proactive regulations being utilized by the government, corporate websites, or mobile apps to make online dating safer?
- Is anyone doing anything in the name of consumer protection? The answer is no—it would be bad for business.

Without delay, reputable dating websites and mobile apps should require their members to submit to a marriage record check, criminal background check, and Open Source Intelligence Search. The effective screening will add an essential layer of protection for those who insist on meeting their mates online. At the same time, cheaters and criminals alike would think twice about using a site that disclosed their convictions for misdemeanors, felonies, and sexual offenses.

And would it really be bad for business? I would submit that growing numbers of people are learning about the dangers of these sites. A few smart, built-in protections would only help a larger clientele feel safer in signing up and paying for such sites.

What is the benefit of screening online daters? Those who have prior misdemeanor and felony convictions or are convicted sexual offenders (Megan's Law) should be allocated a red flag on their online dating profile.

Further, those who are found to be legally married should also be issued a red flag if it isn't disclosed under relationship status. Such a simple, highly visible mark, allocated on the online profile of individuals who bring a criminal history—or who misrepresent their marital status—would go a long way to protect and provide peace of mind to online and mobile daters.

This is in no sense a form of discrimination, but a simple disclosure of public record—we, as citizens, own those records. We have the right to know these things. And we're already showing this wisdom on other fronts. Corporations, for example, have the ability to conduct a background check for marriage and criminal records within 48 hours of the request.

As far as I know, no online matchmaking website currently screens its users. Therefore, criminals have full access to potential victims. With hundreds of millions of adults having tried online dating, how many more victims will we read about—how many more will leave my office in tears—before governments and corporations across the globe will crack down, making online dating safer? How many more will be victimized by a cheater, criminal, or sexual predator?

We should never forget the murders of Adam Hilarie, Jordan Collins, and Katie Locke. Those are the names of three people who were merely looking for love, but who lost their lives due to their use of the online dating site PlentyOfFish.com.

I call upon holding corporations such as InterActiveCorp (Match.com, Tinder, and others) and eHarmony, who are earning millions of dollars profiting from matchmaking, to pay a little attention, and perhaps a little bit of that money, to protect their members. They're likely to find it's not just the right thing to do, but the *profitable* thing to do.

Let's hold these corporations civilly liable. They boast of making a lot of good matches, so shouldn't they own the consequences of the bad ones?

And if you're someone who is considering the use of these sites, my advice is to read this chapter a couple of times and think about the dangers. Before you go wandering into these dark alleys of the Internet, ask yourself if you could be looking for love and entertainment in all the wrong places.

CHAPTER 8
First Lady, We Need to Talk...

"Catching a cheater is a continuous game of cat and mouse...let's play."
Justin Hopson

Everybody wonders about it. *What does Melania Trump think about her husband's alleged affairs?*

After the numbers exceeded a dozen women, the "fake news" defense no longer holds. As a matter of fact, Donald Trump's staunchest defenders don't make denials; they say it doesn't matter. The voters have spoken, and they just don't care about the man's personal life.

But what does Melania think? What does she say to him when they're alone together? Does she talk about it at all?

Who is there to give advice, to offer her a shoulder to cry on?

Has she ever suspiciously peeked at the contacts on her husband's phone?

Has she stood on the other side of a door, listening to his conversations?

As a private investigator, I can't help but wonder if it ever crossed her mind that she could hire someone like me. After all, her husband has hired a few personal consultants in his time; he certainly believes he's entitled to know what's going on. Why shouldn't Melania?

If you've ever wondered how Melania has handled it—or how *you* should—then these pages are the beginning of getting some answers. Answers to the allegations of cheating made by Playboy model, Karen McDougal as well as the porn star, Stephanie Clifford (better known as Stormy Daniels). Not to mention the dozen or so women who've accused

Donald Trump of sexual misconduct...the overt ogling...the unwanted kissing...the unsolicited groping...

> Cast between the shadows of sexual misconduct allegations and assertions—all his own to "grab them by the p*ssy," "The Donald" could be the poster boy for the #MeToo movement.

Believe me, in my work as a private eye, I've seen nearly every situation you can imagine when it comes to adulterous affairs. I've descended into some of the most unpleasant gutters of human interaction, not because I enjoy it at all—I don't—but because it's work somebody must perform. And because I have a disdain for infidelity—*cheating*, as I more often call it, because the act doesn't deserve a formal, fine-sounding vocabulary word. *Cheating* captures it: something dead wrong, something disloyal, and utterly unacceptable to any civil society.

But even for me, the experiences and knowledge foisted upon Melania have been an eye-opener. If these are just the parts we know about, how much remains beneath the tip of the iceberg? I can't help but wonder how many times and to what extent America's 45th President has been cheating on Melania—and his previous wives.

The national media, and many of those who consume it wave all this way. They say, "We don't care who he sleeps with—it's the coverup that matters. It's the campaign financing issue." Or they say anything he does is okay because they support his leadership.

I beg to differ. I make no judgments on the politics; what I'm concerned about here is the message about morality. I'm just old-fashioned enough to believe that cheating matters, and when it happens in high places, it matters even more—because the influence is so much more extensive. The ripples spread out across our entire culture. And even if you ignore the prominence of the man, it still comes back to Melania. She's a human being with feelings. She, along with everyone else personally affected, deserve answers.

I can't predict where their marriage goes from here. In any individual situation, it's unwise to guess. I do know, for solid certainty, that *cheating IS the kiss of death to marriage and monogamous relationships.*

First Lady of The United States, can you hear me?

If so, allow me to introduce myself. My name is Justin Hopson. I am a seasoned private investigator and retired New Jersey State Trooper. Please know that I've been chasing cheaters for over a decade now. In fact, I've had the unenviable task of investigating more than 100 divorce cases and have testified in a fair share of court proceedings.

Having handled the gamut of both criminal and civil cases, my niche is what some refer to as "marital infidelity." But I don't use such formal terminology. *Infidelity, unfaithfulness, and adultery* are too gentle of words, too proper for what they describe. *Cheating* is a better choice, much more direct. If we wink at the things we should condemn and soften our terminology to cushion the blow, we assist in the demise of our family, our community, and our country.

Perhaps I sound intolerant. I won't deny the charge. I'm intolerant of certain things: crimes, acts hurtful of others, and in this case, choices that add up—broken marriages and broken relationships—to devastate children and rip away the fabric that holds modern civilization together: commitment, morality, love.

• • • • • • • • • ● • • • • • • • • • • •

That said, I'm not interested in a diatribe. I write these words to do something positive: to help Melania and millions of other Americans who've been victimized by cheaters. And most importantly of all, to help you make what could be the most important decision of your life: to maintain or cut the relationship that is bringing you pain and confusion.

But this is a book that shouldn't be necessary. Every single one of us deserves better, particularly from those we trust the most. But we all know what's happening around us: marriage isn't getting the respect it must have, and cheaters are abounding. Those who have been betrayed are living in unspeakable pain.

Such people tend to suffer in silence. But when it happens in the White House, it might as well be within a glass house. "Melania cannot do anything. She can't even open a window at the White House. She can't go outside," declared France's First Lady, Brigitte Macron. So everyone knows; everyone reads the most intimate details. Such revelations are deeply unfair, of course. No one deserves humiliation at the highest public level.

Some would say Melania should have read a few headlines before entering into such a marriage. Others would insist, "If she doesn't like it, there's no law against walking away." I'm more sympathetic than that, perhaps because I've known so many people in the throes of heartbreak. I observe Melania Trump as a devoted mother, a loyal wife, a dignified woman, and surely the most beautiful of First Ladies. But nothing in her life prepared her for the sharp spotlight of the world stage.

She obviously desires to live quietly, out of the public eye, but the role of wife to the world's most powerful man has been thrust upon her. I can't begin to imagine the daily pressure she must feel—why else would she publicly wear a jacket scrawled in white lettering, "I REALLY DON'T CARE. DO U?"

Melania Trump deserves an advocate, someone to take a stand on her behalf, someone to discover the truth about her husband's philandering, and someone to advise her on how to respond. In short, she needs someone like me.

If the First Lady hired me, I would begin by saying something like this:

- - - - - - - - - ● - - - - - - - - - -

Melania, no one knows your husband better than you do. No one has observed him in recent days from as close a perspective. As for his past, you've heard all the stories the rest of us have. But it's worth noting that your husband denies each and every charge. He often claims never to have met some of these women.

No matter how unlikely his denials may seem, I would suggest we begin by giving him the benefit of the doubt. Let's be absolutely certain. Therefore our first task is to explore the warning signals that inevitably appear when a spouse or partner is cheating. Have you noticed any of the following red flags that are common in these situations?

- **Your mate suddenly seems to lose interest in your relationship.** There's a new emotional distance that was never there before, and soon it becomes tangible—a physical distance. Your significant other isn't around as much. Once you thought your connection was absolute, but now it seems broken. Sex has dropped off sharply, and you've given up trying to talk about it. Excuses fly, and they have a hollow ring.

- **Though unromantic with you, he seems more interested in his physical appearance than ever.** Cheaters often buy stylish new clothing. They diet and exercise with a new energy that seems to have come out of left field. Why the tattoo? Why the new piercings? None of this seems to be for you, so what's going on?
- **He's very into social media.** In today's world, this innovation tells a fuller story than most of us realize. A spouse who may be cheating suddenly does a lot of posting, particularly of flirtatious pictures. New Facebook friends or Twitter followers suggest a new social circle is out there. Where is your partner meeting all these new people? If you're suspicious, you realize you're married or in a relationship with a stranger.

These are a few of the red flags we look for, but there are others. Consider:

- Projection, or turning the tables. He or she accuses *you* of cheating! This universal sign of guilt, interestingly, has been observed as a frequent practice of Donald Trump.
- A sudden spike in self-centered remarks and behavior.
- Signs of an addictive personality; life is now a constant pleasure trip.
- A noticeable uptick in lying and deception.
- Unexplained (and unexplainable) absences; alibis that don't add up.
- An array of new mobile apps used to conceal, such as the Private Photo app. In this one, the icon is a calculator, but the correct password reveals it to be a cache for secret images. And none of them appear in the phone's primary photo library. Another tool cheaters utilize is simply called Vault. It hides texts, pictures, call logs, and everything else a cheater wants to conceal. It even snaps a quick photo of anyone trying to access it without its owner's

permission. A deceptive mobile app can be the cheater's best friend.
- A strange new tendency for the suspected male to mistreat the other women in his life, including his mother or his sister.

Red flags don't provide direct evidence of cheating any more than smoke is the same as fire. Other factors could be causing strange behavior. Marriage itself, apart from cheating, is complicated and filled with its own bumpy roads and potholes. These indicators, however, suggest that you have reason to take a closer look.

What follows are the facts as I've found them.

CHAPTER 9
The Case Against Donald Trump

"When I think of the person that I thought was Bill Clinton, I think he had genuine remorse. When I think of the person that I now see is 100 percent politician, I think he's sorry he got caught." Monica Lewinsky

Once we know something very serious and very wrong is going on, where do we go from there? It's time to examine the specifics of the case and begin to gather real evidence that cheating is occurring.

First, unpleasant as the task may be, we need to follow the "hush money" trail.

As you know, for many years your husband used an attorney who was, in fact, more of a "fixer." His name is Michael Cohen, and he's been known to issue threats to news outlets that were planning stories on Donald Trump's behavior.

He also worked with publishers such as *The National Enquirer*, owned by a friend of your husband's. Cohen arranged for the periodical to buy all rights to a story, then promptly bury it from the public's view. This common practice is called "catch and kill," and it shields improper sexual behavior from the public's eyes—including yours. This was the case with Karen McDougal, who later sued because she never intended her story to be hidden away.

Cohen has also used simple cash payoffs for signed agreements, binding the sex partner to silence about the affair. He used this strategy with the porn star, Stormy Daniels. In an interview for the book *Fire and*

Fury, your husband's strategist Steve Bannon alleged that Cohen used his "fixer" skills with "one hundred" women during the presidential campaign. This may well be an exaggeration, but it indicates a chronic pathology of womanizing. A few women have come forward nonetheless, but how many more are out there?

I submit to you, Melania, that Donald Trump has provided sufficient motive, opportunity, and evidence for us to demonstrate his lifestyle of cheating. The fact that Michael Cohen pled guilty in federal court to violations tied to payments that he made or orchestrated to porn star Stormy Daniels and Playboy model Karen McDougal is, in fact, a significant legal footprint into your husband's infidelity.

Motive

When I investigate the possibility of adultery in a divorce case, I must begin with inclination or motive. We need to prove a spouse was inclined to have sex with an adulterous partner, and of course, this is done by presenting evidence of sexual desire between the two.

What kinds of evidence? Explicit love letters. Emails. Texts. Internet posts of various sorts. Though hacking is illegal, a private eye may utilize software to access profile information such as photographic timelines and locales. Somewhere there's likely to be the evidence we need because those in wild pursuit of sexual conquest will often be reckless in their behavior.

As an investigator, I check telephone records and scour credit card statements with consent from the joint account holder. Finally, eyewitness accounts of romantic behavior—kissing or holding hands, perhaps in a restaurant or the walk to a car afterward—will clinch the case that a line has been crossed and an affair is in progress.

In the case of Donald Trump, nearly everyone has, by now, seen photographs in which he poses with a woman who later admits to an affair. Without these pictures, the president might have claimed never to have met Karen McDougal, as he has done in other cases. We know that he took great precautions to cover the woman's tracks when a rendezvous was scheduled. Cohen or bodyguard Keith Schiller would make careful, non-trackable arrangements; false names were often used.

Still, a photograph cropped up and established the illicit couple's presence at a certain place and a certain time.

One particular night, the president-to-be asked his son, Eric, to pick out the most beautiful girl at the Playboy Mansion. According to Karen McDougal, Eric selected her, the father grinned and congratulated Eric on his "great taste."

Clumsiness abounding; inclination established.

Opportunity

Opportunity must exist for a misdeed to be possible. This is why alibis are established—or at least attempted. Donald Trump claimed several times not to have stayed overnight in Moscow on an important visit, but flight records, an FBI Director, and photographs debunked his alibi. Whether or not he was involved with prostitutes as claimed, of course, is an open question, but it's clear that he lied on the matter of opportunity. Consequently, he would later admit on a morning talk show that he "stayed there (Russia) for a short period of time, but of course, I stayed there." In today's world, it's more difficult to move around without leaving an information trail. For celebrities, it's nearly impossible.

We pursue evidence that a spouse was alone with his or her lover in a private place for enough time to consummate an affair. If I can demonstrate that a husband spent considerable time at a specific woman's house, for example, I've shown opportunity.

Still, the courts expect more than vague accusations that something must have happened during that interval. Proof must be "sufficiently definite to establish place and time." In other words, were these two people indisputably alone together for this time on that date? I might establish the husband parking his car at a girlfriend's house at 9:00 p.m. If the vehicle remains in place until 3:00 a.m., when he emerges and drives away, I have strong proof of opportunity.

Evidence

Adultery is a private act by its very nature. It occurs behind closed doors, and nearly always away from prying eyes. For this reason, courts allow the circumstantial evidence. If I needed to provide an eyewitness to a sexual act, I would never be able to prove my case. Other kinds of evidence, therefore, come into play.

Friends may be called upon to provide written statements, or to testify in court about the details of an affair. We might present photographs and communications records (such as text logs or phone archives) to the judge. What about a personal investigation—"tailing" your husband or wife? Your attorney is likely to strongly advise that you avoid inviting danger or trouble with privacy laws. However, a licensed private investigator might help you get to the truth.

Every situation is unique. In the case of investigating a wealthy celebrity and later a president such as Donald Trump, advantages and disadvantages are fairly obvious. Any affair occurring within 1600 Pennsylvania Avenue itself would be difficult to investigate because the White House is the most heavily protected building in the world. On the other hand, Mr. Trump's movements are documented and continuously photographed. The press and paparazzi serve as de facto investigators who are never off duty.

But Melania, I would remind you that you're closer to your husband than anyone else, with the possible exception of his Secret Service detail. There are ways for you to get information—if you're willing to get your hands a little "dirty."

Let me explain what I mean by that phrase. If you suspect cheating is ongoing, and you want to be proactive in gathering evidence, this is the starting point for deciding about what future the two of you might have as a married couple.

You would begin by keeping a written chronology. Times moves quickly. Details are lost to memory unless we carefully record them for posterity. On the old show Dragnet, Sergeant Joe Friday used to say, "Just the facts, ma'am." I would say the same to you. Write down the who, what, when, where and how of everything that happens regarding your husband.

You ask, "How do I know what's important?"

If you're not sure, write it down anyway. What seems insignificant today might be a building block to our future construction of the truth. Attorneys, law enforcement, judges, and juries will appreciate every piece of information you can turn over to them. Your written records will also refresh your recollections.

Now for the computer. You may not be surprised to learn that the Internet has become one of the primary tools of cheaters who may use dating sites, chat rooms, or social media simply to meet potential romantic partners. We think of these sites and apps as socially convenient, but they're helpful in other ways, too. They track movements across the Internet, just as GPS devices do across the map.

Your browser—Microsoft Explorer or Edge, Google Chrome or Firefox, for example—keep logs within their settings, usually under "history." Take note of dating or chat sites your husband might have visited, and how frequently. Keep in mind that your husband may not tell you a password and may also purge the history (Internet cache) frequently.

Even if you don't find the proverbial "smoking gun," you might at least come up with a red flag. A sharp spike in social media points to a sudden increase in social activity. People may obscure their Internet activity for a variety of reasons—some of them entirely valid—but if you find this happening, it's at least reason enough to maintain your suspicions.

Special Internet history trackers are useful. The spouse may be covering his or her trail and feel a false sense of security; meanwhile, the tracker avoids those filters. It sends you a report of any online movements. Print out all reports for your records, and keep them in a safe, hidden place.

If and when you've documented, through an Internet tracker, your husband's activities on dating, chat, or pornographic sites on more than one occasion, the time has probably come to clear the air. This, of course, is a tense and crucial moment. Before broaching such an explosive subject, think about what you're going to say. Prepare your words and demeanor calmly, make sure your emotions are in check (as emotional as this subject is), and have your activity history in front of you.

Then find the best time to say something like, "Is it okay if we talk? I need you to tell me if you've been visiting inappropriate websites."

Since this sudden suggestion may take your significant other by surprise, you have an opportunity to observe visual indicators such as body language, facial expression, a tone of voice, and other signboards of the truth, above and beyond any words that are offered.

It's harder to be a convincing liar than people often assume, particularly when taken off guard. Some people are better liars than others.

Unprepared lies are the most revealing. They cause people to alter what they say and how they say it, in ways that are highly noticeable to those who know them well. Sociopaths may lie masterfully, but short of that, your spouse is likely to showcase his deception, shame, and embarrassment.

Once you've asked the initial question, you're likely to get back something like this: "No! Why would you ask me such a question?"

Or, in the case of someone bolder: "So what if I do visit a few sites? Isn't that my own business?"

Show your copies of the tracker's report. You might say, "If you have nothing to hide, I'm sure you won't mind sharing your passwords."

If you've uncovered a secret, then don't be surprised by a fight-or-flight reaction, and you might see both. Lie-and-deny is the quickest option. Another will be twisting the issue into, "Instead of some trivial web site, we ought to be talking about why you don't trust me." This is the fight option. It's likely to be followed by storming out of the room and slamming a door—the flight response. A show of anger is meant to obscure the genuine guilt and shame of being caught.

Knowing your spouse well, you'll have an accurate prediction of the reaction you'll get. That anticipation will help you to be prepared and to respond wisely rather than reactively, falling into the obvious traps that allow him to escape the issue. Game-plan the confrontation, including holding your emotions in reserve. Be prepared with the right words and responses at the right times.

Always take a look at your mate's smartphone. This is the invention that has come to dominate our social lives, and mobile phones have quite a story to tell about their owner. They're the modern version of the cigarette, giving us something to hold in our hands and toy with...this new addiction is changing our lives more than we know. Cell phones were introduced to make our lives simpler, and of course, they've had the opposite effect.

These tiny "central command posts" for our lives are motherlodes of private information, and quite valuable for catching a cheating spouse. Personal videos, pictures, correspondences, communications, information searches, personal info, e-commerce—all these are stored in the tiny devices we carry in our pockets. So watch how closely your significant other guards that phone. It might be one of the most significant red flags of all.

If your husband continually texts by stepping away from your eyeshot or earshot, you have every right to ask what's going on. What if your spouse carries the phone everywhere, including to the bathroom, and keeps it right beside the pillow at night? What if he reacts quickly and with barely concealed panic if you happen to pick up that phone? That's when you know something is wrong.

While your husband is talking quietly on the phone, and you walk right up, what happens? Does he begin to speak more softly? Does he abruptly end the call? Does he glance at the phone and say, "I'll check that later," shoving the phone back in his pocket, when a text message or email arrives while you're nearby?

Secretive phone behavior has become a recognizable behavior pattern, and it declares that someone has secrets. But that's not to say that you can't have a secret of your own—such as, hypothetically, turning on and monitoring your husband's smartphone location through its "Find My Phone" app.

You've probably heard about an even more modern innovation, the "burner phone." These are inexpensive, prepaid devices that might be picked up at a convenience store, ideal for private, untraceable conversations during a short period of time. They're unregistered and therefore secure, even from the law. But they're still physical items. They must be stored somewhere, and with a little thought, you'll have some good ideas where: the car's glove compartment or beneath the seat; in a briefcase; the hidden pocket of a raincoat; the drawer of the study or someplace the spouse frequents. It may be "throwaway," but it must be stowed away. Once found, it will reveal what numbers it's been used to call, and needless to say, this is significant evidence.

Credit cards and bank statements should be scrutinized as well. If they show unfamiliar restaurants, hotels, and retail charges, then make extra copies of all records. Be sure to check the unfamiliar records against the written chronology you've been keeping.

The more angles you look into, the better view you'll have of the big picture. And one other thing: Trust your instincts. You probably know your mate quite well, and the mind absorbs more signals and cues than we realize. Intuition is very often the mind's ability to take all kinds of information and distill it into a "gut level" hunch that the physical evidence will bear out.

Know also that the best tool an investigator has is pure objectivity. You might not want the truth to be what it is. You might yearn for your significant other to be completely innocent, and if so, you'll leap at any clue that points to innocence.

Denial is a powerful refuge, but it's a dangerous place to live. Think rationally and honestly. Be willing to look closely at whatever picture is revealed, whether you want it to appear or not. Merely follow the clues where they lead. It may be painful for a time, but as the Bible says, the truth shall set you free. Choose truth.

- - - - - - - - - ● - - - - - - - - - -

So Melania, there you have it. I've laid out the basics of how I help my clients launch personal investigations. Though your situation is unique and complex, your best course is to quietly, discreetly begin to open your eyes, watch and observe, and collect the evidence available to you.

Let's assume, just for the sake of these pages, you've come away with a handful of red flags. Motive, opportunity, and evidence seem to be present. Much of the secretive behavior I've outlined above has intruded into your relationship.

In that event, hiring me would be a worthy investment. You're caught up in something you never dreamed you'd have to face. Your head is spinning, and your emotions are in turmoil. There are no stormier waters to navigate in life (no pun intended). You need assistance, and it needs to be very skilled. You'll get one shot at this.

An experienced private investigator has walked this road more than a few times. He is objective, he's on the outside, and he majors in problem-solving. What you're facing feels like the end of the world to you, but a PI deals with these things all the time.

Since I'm not a part of your life or your husband's, I can deal solidly and efficiently with the problem. I have no biases, emotionally or otherwise. And I know the best resources and strategies.

I approach every situation as a large picture broken into many puzzle pieces. The task is to gather those pieces, one by one, and assemble them into the one image that solves the puzzle. I know from experience I'll gather many pieces that don't go with this picture at all—they're part of some other image. Our lives are not isolated paintings, but galleries full of different pictures. You have many life circles and areas; so does your spouse. My skill is in knowing how to sort out the many pieces, find the ones we're looking for, and discard the others. Once we have the full picture, we can present it convincingly to a judge and jury.

As a licensed PI, one who has assembled many pictures, I know each case well enough to fully document the infidelity and testify powerfully to it in court. Thus, the financial investment to the PI may result in far more considerable sums of money saved for the future, based on alimony and other settlements.

I mentioned that word *licensed*. I strongly recommend working with someone experienced and accredited. Each state has some extent of regulations and oversight that licensed private investigators adhere to. These should be bonded, insured, and provide a written contract prior to conducting the investigation.

Could you use more than one PI at the outset? Why not? You could hear from *Magnum PI* and then get a second opinion, straight from the *Rockford Files* (assuming you know your old TV shows). We seek second opinions from doctors to make sure we get an accurate diagnosis. A possibly cheating spouse is a serious "condition," too. There's no reason you can't speak to several different private investigators before going ahead with a surveillance operation.

It's a big decision, and it's also a financial one, so you'll want to go into it intelligently.

* * * * * * * * ● * * * * * * * * * * *

So if you are scratching your head wondering how I'll do it—that is, what actions I take to catch a cheater, then pay attention. Everybody's curious about this part. They've seen a few TV shows and movies, and they envision fistfights and car chases down dark streets. Spoiler alert: Real-life isn't always like television.

I do know the basics of my work. I don't have space to lay out every one of them, but I can give you a crash course.

It begins and ends with hard evidence, as you can imagine. And the most potent form of proof is a perpetrator caught in the act. That's why surveillance is the best strategy for catching a cheating spouse with exception, of course, to the POTUS. Later on, I'll tell you a couple of stories that illustrate what that's like. Stay tuned for chapters six and seven as I take you behind the lens of my surveillance camera. You'll have a front row seat to see how video and still photography of adulterous activity is unbeatable evidence in a court of law. Judges and juries respond to incriminating images because cases are no longer about "he said, she said."

You've heard it said that "it's not what you know, but what you can prove." You might have figured out the who, the what, the where, and the when. You may even have seen it with your own two eyes. Your spouse may also have admitted the whole thing. But once you're both in the courtroom, he might sing a different tune. Judges and juries don't know what you know. You're going to need objective, tangible evidence.

A good PI will make use of every possible resource, and in today's world, there are more than ever before. We've mentioned a number of these, but there are many more. We keep up with new developments in technology because highly useful resources enter the world constantly. If we're paying attention, we can keep a step ahead of targets everywhere—even Donald Trump. Right now, someone in Silicon Valley is sure to be working on yet another innovation.

For example, take ride-sharing services such as Uber and Lyft—a highly successful, available, and affordable taxi or private car transportation service. At any hour of the day, someone with an app on his or her phone can summon a driver and get an affordable ride.

What does this have to do with cheaters? They see such services as opportunities to outfox the rest of us. They worry about being followed, or if they're thinking even more seriously, about having their movements monitored by GPS. Uber and Lyft seem less traceable. They might also want to give the appearance of being where they're not, by leaving a personal car at the home or office. What they fail to consider is that they're leaving one more clear trail—even sending out an alert of where they are and where they're going, by way of the smartphone app that signals the services.

And consider this: What if a private investigator moonlights as an independent contractor for Uber or Lyft? Stranger things have happened. Some PIs are that clever and that aggressive.

During surveillance operations, private investigators tend to be near a target. If a suspected cheater calls Uber or Lyft for a ride, the PI, who also may be a labor contractor for ride-sharing services, receives an alert and can respond accordingly. These services are a boon to the PI who has a handy way to monitor, follow, or even drive the suspected cheater to the "scene of the crime."

In your case, Melania, your husband utilizes the Secret Service, not Uber. So I'd angle towards getting affidavits from his previous chauffeurs, boat captains, pilots, and travel associates. The purpose of the affidavits is to expose person(s) of interest who had an inappropriate physical or emotional connection with your husband.

Yes, I know about the famous nondisclosure agreements. The fact that someone like Donald Trump uses these almost reflexively is a red flag in itself. But even with signed contracts, we find many people who are eager to report impropriety.

Once pertinent names for my investigation are obtained, I'd conduct comprehensive background checks. Liens, lawsuits, judgments, and other information provide a vivid picture and can be used to further the case.

You're in search of the truth, and beyond that, at least the possibility of ending your marriage—telling Donald Trump, "You're fired." In that case—demonstrating adultery—you must meet a high standard of proof that will hold up in court. We'll continue to talk about what that entails throughout this book.

I would submit multiple Freedom of Information Act requests (FOIA) to gain access to government records. Consequently, I would collect evidence specific to conflicting statements made by Donald Trump, attorney(s) representing Donald Trump, Michael Cohen, and attorney(s) representing Michael Cohen. My approach to obtain tangible evidence vis-à-vis payments given to alleged mistresses is pertinent to my investigation. Evidence such as Donald Trump's 2017 financial disclosure form, which confirms he made a payment to Cohen between $100,001 and $250,000 in 2016 (presumably "hush money" for pornographic film actress, Stephanie Clifford). Riddle me this: *Why pay someone for something they didn't do?*

Then I would talk with as many of your husband's associates as possible. You'd be amazed at the ripple effect we can create by doing that. Create enough of a ripple, bring in enough friends, and somebody might even finally feel a bit of embarrassment and even shame—that's when the plot thickens!

CHAPTER 10
Cheat and Repeat

"History repeats itself, but in such cunning disguise that we never detect the resemblance until the damage is done." ~ Sidney J. Harris

If the First Lady hired me, I would tell her how honored I was; then I would approach her like any client. I'd seek to understand as much as possible about her life and experience.

The backstory: I realize that for many years, Melania was seen by the public merely as a celebrity's trophy wife, an ornament on the arm of a flamboyant, headline-stealing icon. But in November 2016, she suddenly found herself cast in the role of America's First Lady—against all the odds and indeed against any of her own stated desires…her life would change forever.

America was now fascinated to learn more about the mystery woman with striking beauty and a quiet presence. Melania Knauss was born on April 26, 1970, in the town of Sevnica, which is found in Slovenia, south of Austria and east of Italy. She was born with distinct beauty to the extent that she was entered in fashion shows at the age of five by her parents. There is no culture across the globe that doesn't appreciate physical beauty in women, elevating the loveliest and most desirable in order to satisfy the fascination of others.

At sixteen she appeared in television commercials; by eighteen, she had signed with a top modeling agency in Milan, Italy. And in her mid-twenties, she made the ultimate move in fashion circles, relocating to New York City and being placed by her handlers in an apartment at Union

IF THE FIRST LADY HIRED ME...

Square, where a male photographer watched over her and showed her the ropes.

We might expect a young and glamorous woman to have flowed smoothly into the glitzy nightlife of the Big Apple. But she behaved in a more introverted way, less disposed to making friends or hanging out at nightclubs other than the times it was suggested or required. We can imagine the culture shock of Times Square after being raised in a small town in central Europe. Not everyone thrives on such a frantic transition.

When Melania sought male companionship, it was notably with older men—father figures, perhaps—and only for dinner. She avoided staying out late, and relationships were never long-lasting since her agency kept her on the road for photo shoots.

Young models, especially those imported from smaller countries, are heavily pressured to maintain the perfect physique, the flawless skin, and the ideal hair. Melania walked around in ankle weights. She ate a diet of fruit and vegetables, drank gallons of water, and sought that payday that might someday, somehow give her the freedom to choose her own path. She knew this was a life that burst into bright light, only to flame out quickly.

American society glamorizes the supermodel, the sudden starlet chosen for the cover of the Sports Illustrated Swimsuit Edition or the latest Victoria's Secret model to sashay down the runway. We shower them with money, attention, and admiration. It never occurs to us to consider the pressure that comes with such a role; the fleeting nature of the worship. A few years, a few wrinkles, and yesterday's goddess is discarded for a newer version. Melania understood the rules. The clock was running, and in due course, the checks would grow smaller and then scarce. Then perhaps she'd find herself stranded in New York City with far fewer friends and opportunities, or simply deported to her home country with few options.

Even then, Melania couldn't seem to climb to the top of the heap. Other models quickly surpassed her popularity and demand. Her agency was growing impatient. She worked, but only at second- and third-tier modeling jobs. At some point, the company investment in her would yield diminishing returns. There were whispers that she was "stiff," statuesque but lacking in that sparkling, vivacious x-factor that marked the top models.

But one day she attended a party—one more Manhattan evening, one more cocktail gathering. Zampolli, her agency, threw it at the Kit Kat Club at Times Square. This was September 1998, the year Melania turned 28. The billionaire Donald Trump was there, with Norwegian cosmetics heiress Celina Midelfart on his arm, and his always roving eye caught sight of Melania. As soon as his date was excused to the restroom, he wasted no time approaching the young lady and asking for her phone number. Melania, showing a spark of independence, insisted on taking his number instead.

It wasn't long before the two were seen in public as an item on the social gossip agenda. Trump was in the midst of a notorious, ugly divorce. Melania took her share of kidding, because even then—particularly in New York—Trump was seen as something of a comic figure. Was it his wild mop of hair that attracted her or his constant monologue?

No, she protested—no, he was a "real man," the ultimate older father figure. Melania seemingly wanted someone with the power, presence, and authority to walk through a confusing cultural world.

For Trump himself, it just happened to be the right timing as the marriages with Ivana and Marla were behind him now. His bride-to-be, Melania, was not only beautiful—she kept a quiet distance. She respected his space.

But it took more than five years before the couple tied the knot. They married in 2005, with a predictably lavish party at Mar-a-Lago. Celebrities, media figures, and politicians were everywhere. Then they settled into the marriage that comes with the Trump Dynasty.

Six months after the wedding, Melania was expecting their child. But she was no longer 28; she was now 35, the dreaded "checkout time" he had publicly declared on a radio show. They were still newlyweds, strictly speaking, but his roving eye was particularly busy in 2005. His wife was building a nest; he was spreading his wings to fly.

During this time, of course, he was becoming more famous through his hit TV show, *The Apprentice*, and perhaps it's fair to suggest that fame made him even more pompous and brash. In time, he was receiving one million dollars per episode, and he was given a star on the Hollywood

Walk of Fame. Yet for years he had talked about the ultimate power trip—running for President of the United States.

Once he did run for president, of course, the accusations began to emerge. The very year he and Melania were married, according to one account, allegedly he had sexually assaulted a female reporter at Mar-a-Lago while his wife was in the next room. The notorious *Access Hollywood* tape, in which he discussed his predatory attitude toward women in offensive terms, was made that same year of 2005. The time frame never seemed to matter—whether at one of his beauty pageants or at work, whether on the set of his TV show or on a trip, he seemingly sought out sexual conquests. More than a dozen women eventually came forward to report his approaches, with their various degrees of success. In some cases, the women recounted asking Trump, "What about your wife?" He seemed always to reply, "Don't worry about her."

Of twelve allegations of unwanted physical contact, five—nearly half—occurred in 2005 or 2006, the period in which he was setting up a household with Melania and becoming a dad again.

Trump has called each and every one of his accusers a liar. In one case, during the 2016 presidential campaign, he stood before the crowd and ridiculed an accuser's looks, asking the crowd whether they thought a man like him would waste his time with someone not up to his standards of beauty.

Again, upon hearing these things, I wondered what Melania was thinking about all of it. The nature of her Old-World upbringing couldn't have prepared her for these things—but we've observed a stoicism in Melania, a quiet strategy of bearing up and making the most of her life that she could. She's clearly a devoted mother and someone who enjoys visiting schools and chatting with students.

It's quite fascinating that as First Ladies often select a pet "cause," hers is none other than "Be Best" and specifically cyberbullying—while being married to arguably the world's most prominent cyberbully. We can't help but wonder whether the irony is unconscious, or whether she's making a statement in her own indirect way.

There may be two women in this world who truly understand. Their names are Marla and Ivana. Each of these gave Donald Trump at least one child. Each was courted, sported around, and dispatched unceremoniously in due time. And by the time Melania came along, a pattern had developed—history repeating itself. Cheat, repeat.

Trump married Ivana Zelnickova, his first wife, in 1977. During the eighties, he began keeping his mistress, Marla Maples, in a hotel room near Trump Tower. At one point he went on a vacation to Aspen, Colorado with Ivana, and tried keeping his mistress nearby without his wife finding out. Finally, Marla walked up to Mrs. Trump at the resort and said, "I love Donald. Do you?"

After the affair became public, Trump decided to bask in the attention. To him, there was no such thing as bad publicity. The ensuing divorce negotiations, loud and messy, captivated a celebrity-obsessed culture.

Regardless of his supposedly unlimited field of conquest, he tied the knot with one woman again, this time with Marla Maples in 1993. Their daughter Tiffany was already two months old. As usual, the wedding was an "everybody who's anybody" event with hundreds of guests including (ironically) Rosie O'Donnell. But within a few years, this match, too, ended in divorce. By this time, of course, Trump had found Melania, though there were other women along the way. Like Ivana before her, Marla accepted her settlement and went her own way. That settlement, of course, tightly bound her to silence.

It's unlikely that any future biographer will figure out who holds the dubious honor of being Donald Trump's first affair. But these liaisons have been so much a part of his public life—old dogs perform the same old tricks.

The result of this is that our illustrious hall of presidents now has its first entry who is thrice-married, with children by each marriage; with pending sexual assault lawsuits; and with the most beautiful and visibly least happy First Lady in memory. This was underlined on the night of Donald Trump's first State of the Union address. As new stories circulated about her husband's affairs, she rode separately to the U. S. Capitol, rather than arriving in the same car. No one could remember anything like that with previous presidents. She had also canceled out on attending an important international trip beside her husband.

These refusals were enough to cause quite a few whispers, and for once, everyone was fairly certain what Melania was thinking.

・・・・・・・・●・・・・・・・・・・

If the First Lady hired me, I would ask her to think about all these things; to consider the two courses set before her. The first would be to "stand by her man" and hope for the best. Perhaps he'll change. We all want to believe people can grow and live more wisely. Maybe he'll fall in love with her all over again.

The other path, then, is to think about happiness. Think about freedom. Think about the best life for the many years ahead. She is still a young woman, still capable of doing great things, given the public platform she now has. There is one service she could undoubtedly offer to the world. That service would be "modeling" again, this time holding out to the world a model of refusing to accept the humiliation that has been doled out to her. In other words, she could choose the path of standing up and walking out.

To stay, to cling to marriage—there's a certain courage inherent in that. It's the old-fashioned value of honoring marriage. But at what cost? This woman has one life to be happy. And how many others, struggling through relational distrust are watching? How many need the encouragement to stand up and take back their own lives and destinies?

As First Lady and First Divorcee, she would gain tremendous power. She could say to the world, "This is still a nation that is all about family, commitment, and integrity. Cheating will not be tolerated. It's un-American, and I won't allow it."

Melania, are you open to what I have to say?

CHAPTER 11
Divine Intervention

Above all, love each other deeply, because love covers over a multitude of sins.
1 Peter 4:8

When you get down to brass tacks, the idea of marriage has one glaring problem: the people within it. When two ordinary human beings, filled with ordinary flaws, issues, and blind spots come together, what else should we expect but the mingling of one group of problems exacerbated by another?

It is safe to say that Melania ignored the warning signals in Donald's character, maybe she figured that she could "fix him." The fact is that none of us are perfect, but we hope our mate will love us warts and all. Can we make that happen, then maintain it over the course of a long life together? Marriage is a marathon, not a sprint.

This is why Melania Knauss and Donald Trump looked each other right in the eye, before God and community, and said something like, "From this day forward, for better or for worse." It needs to be solemn. It needs to be in the form of a sacred vow. And we need to have a circle of witnesses because the idea is that they hold us accountable for what is perhaps life's hardest work and most glorious reward.

If the First Lady Hired Me and honored me with her trust and openness, which, needless to say, I need if I'm going to do my work effectively, she'd have to share the backstory of her marriage…revealing red flags. Why? Infidelity isn't like some asteroid that plummets out of the blue sky with no warning, no good reason, crushing us on the sidewalk "just because."

IF THE FIRST LADY HIRED ME...

It's the result of a process, a chain reaction of wrong turns, unmet needs, unheeded warnings.

Sometimes—a lot of times, actually—my clients only come to fully understand that process as they sit down and tell me their stories at length. The tears flow as they finally grasp the hard truth even as they speak it to me. I wince at the pain they're feeling as if it were my own because over time I've seen too many people feel that hurt.

I've seen, over and over, a cross-section of the terrible American trend of husbands failing to step up and take leadership within their families.

How many times have you heard this? "Well," says a husband. "Let me ask the boss." It's said only half-seriously, but that half tells us something; a lot of truth is said in jest. Men sometimes gripe about not calling the shots, but of course, it often happens because they're not taking the responsibility that puts someone in the position to call the shots.

Even commercials and sitcoms often portray American husbands as Homer Simpson: potbellied, lovably useless, aw-shucks males. Just look at the stature of American husbands on many TV commercials, and you'll understand why the term "Dad Bod" was coined. As a husband and father, myself, I don't find it cute. I find it very troubling as a snapshot of a nation that is supposed to be the greatest in the world.

I bring all this up in a book about adultery because, at some point, we have to ask whether it's another reason so many married women are having affairs these days. Traditionally we've focused on the male in the workplace, and the classic situation is his affair with an unmarried secretary. But studies suggest that more than fifty percent of married women have an affair at some point. As a matter of fact, since 2012 my business has seen a noticeable uptick in women cheating on men. I suppose the *Mad Men* world of the late fifties is long behind us.

We tend to blame it all on more working women, but from my many conversations and my own judgment of the world around me, I don't think women have changed. They still long for a sense of strength and security from their husbands, and I also believe that kind of husband is on the endangered species list.

One way or another, men are having affairs, women are doing the same, and the traditional marriage is in a state of chaos. It certainly wouldn't hurt for more men to embrace strong leadership and fidelity in their families. That takes a high degree of self-sacrifice, rather than the selfishness that I find at the center of every case of adultery.

Cheaters, I've discovered, haven't thought much about the feelings of their mates. They're wrapped up in their desires; intensely selfish.

••••••••••●•••••••••

When I met the Morrison's, I'd have said they were in hot pursuit of the American Dream—except they'd already seemed to have caught it.

A million-dollar home on a golf course. Four beautiful children. Two careers in medicine (husband and wife were both doctors). All the conventional measurements of success were in place, yet that family was close to collapse.

In a coffee shop, I met Annette V. Morrison, MD in order to hear about her life. It was a story filled with alcohol addiction, self-loathing, and a well-publicized cheating scandal. In the past were the glimmerings of a good marriage, but it had faded away with the onslaught of bad decisions and sad moments of self-destruction. But all roads led back to Dr. Morrison's deep-rooted conviction that she just wasn't good enough and never would be.

It began, best as I could tell, during her middle school years, when the world seems to revolve around petty things—particularly personal appearance. She was developmentally inferior to her peers. Much later in life, Annette would come to understand that she had an addictive personality. But it was too early for that kind of self-understanding and combined with her lack of self-confidence, ordinary happiness eluded her.

She was one of those ostracized kids, the ones picked on, unpopular, unchosen for the good parties and cliques. Some kids, the ones with some special inner strength, shake it off, make social headway later, and show no ill effects. Solid family support helps, and Annette had that. Still, she was devastated by her rejection at the hands of her middle school peers.

Life doesn't wait for us to get it all together inside. It moves on—to full adolescence, perhaps to college, to adulthood, maybe even (in Annette's case) medical school. Beyond that, marriage and family. People see our progress and confuse it with personal growth. But the adult with every social attainment may still be plagued with issues best resolved many years ago. They never surrender quietly. Inner turmoil ultimately manifests itself on the outside.

Annette V. Morrison excelled academically and assimilated well during her medical residency, and tried to keep her eyes on the future. Grades came easy; people did not. In college, she explored the life of the "bad girl," and tried to shed the image of the teacher's pet. She had a few sexual liaisons, tried a few episodes of binge drinking, and wondered if these were the requirements of "fitting in."

I picked up on certain familiar cues. "Do you have a family history of addiction?" I asked.

"My family? No—not at all. The last thing I ever wanted was for them to know about some of my problems. I wouldn't have told them for anything in the world."

She seemed to be searching for something she couldn't find—some type of activity that would tell her everything was all right, that she had the right look or the right style or whatever it took to be a socially acceptable human being. First, it was cigarettes. Then she pursued pornography, alcohol, money, and finally sex.

"I was having sex with fellow residents like it was a carousel," she told me.

By now she was married, living in the mansion, mothering those four children. How many people would have loved to have been Dr. Annette Morrison? Would have concluded they had everything they needed for a happy life? But she was a prestigious, wealthy emergency room doctor caught in a cycle of self-destructive affairs.

Annette Morrison was a functioning alcoholic in the midst of an ongoing affair with a co-worker. I sat and watched her order her coffee black with extra sugar, and I nodded my head, adding it up with what I knew about her. Caffeine. Sugar. Whatever extra stimulation is available for consumption. These are the marks of the addictive personality.

"Yes, that's me," she said as I pointed out the obvious. During the previous year, her suppressed issues had finally ganged up on her. She'd blasted with 'truth bombs' in the form of painful confessions, struggles of faith vs. doubt, and occasional bouts of rage. On a daily basis, she was drinking straight vodka, cigarette in the other hand always lit, eyes restlessly checking the horizon for the next misbegotten rush.

Her husband didn't know about the "guy on the side." What she told herself was that he was an escape valve, a way to let off a little steam from the pressures of a high-pressure daily job coupled with the regular challenges of having four kids and a husband. In other words, she rationalized it all in the normal ways that will convince nobody else—including ourselves, in the end. She accounted for the fact it was wrong, that she'd have guilt. She'd get her life straight later.

What she didn't account for was the grapevine.

· · · · · · · · · · ● · · · · · · · · · · ·

Hospital staffs are like every other corridor. They're made of people who gossip, and gossip travels at a rapid speed and doesn't care whose ears it reaches—including those of the families it concerns.

That's when things finally began to fall apart.

She admitted to the affair and threw in the addictions. It was time to bring everything out into the light and try making a clean break with the problems that were consuming her from the inside out. She took a leave of absence from the hospital and entered a rehab program. The time apart from home, husband, kids, and career were bittersweet.

"I needed to center myself," she said. "I needed to find out what life looked like through sober eyes."

How exactly do we "center" ourselves? Around what, exactly? Annette Morrison found that with God, the center would hold. She needed to be accountable to her oath as a physician, to her husband as a mate, to her children as a mother. But also to God, as a child inside still stuck in unresolved adolescent pain. She believes that if not for divine intervention, she would have destroyed everything and every relationship in her life. And who but God could have overcome the long-entrenched voices of negativity and self-loathing inside her?

"I had feelings of hopelessness, insecurity, and thoughts of suicide, all through my affair and addiction. But now everything has changed. I cling to God's promises of redemption and restoration," she says, and I see the clarity in her eyes. She means it. "My family would have been forever torn apart by my self-destructive behavior—the ravages of a life of compounded sin."

• • • • • • • • ● • • • • • • • • • •

In a book as deadly serious as this one, I wanted to tell the truth—but the whole truth, which includes the possibility of hope and redemption. I have to be honest and say that nothing will destroy a marriage like infidelity and that in most cases, it's a point of no return. I've seen many couples try to put things back together again, but a shattered marriage is so much like glass. The breakage is too complete, and the pieces are too sharp.

If you're planning to commit adultery, that's a decision that's on you. Nobody can stop you. Just don't tell yourself that once you've done it, you can undo the damage. Know that damage will be done and it will be profound including to your own soul and your own outward life. Because once you break that trust, the odds will never be in your favor for rebuilding it.

But yes, there are also the Morrison's. Annette's story is there to remind us that nothing is quite impossible. There is hope, but it must be found in something larger than ourselves. It has to be something that provides a powerful center, around which a whole new life can be built. And it can't be done unilaterally. Spouse and children are part of it, too. Annette had a husband who was willing to forgive and to fight for the family they'd built.

Tim Kimmel may have said it best, "Even with the disappointments... raising children is still the greatest thing you'll ever do. It's greater than any milestone you can hit in your career. It dwarfs any fame you may receive for your ideas or your inventions. You've been handed a piece of history in advance—a gracious gift you send to a time you will not see—and you play the biggest role in how that history will ultimately be recorded."

Annette tells me the Morrison's are closer-knit than ever, finally a happy family. They cling to faith as the tie that binds them to each other and to a life that has beaten the odds and persists toward that elusive happy ending. Her inner demons are finally silenced, and her eyes are set on a far more peaceful horizon, one built around a solid foundation, a loving family, and the solid belief that she's as good as anyone else.

So if in fact, Donald Trump has made the gravest mistake in matrimony by cheating on Melania, will he admit to it? Will divine intervention take shape in the Trump dynasty similar to the Morrison Family? Only time will tell...anything is possible with forgiveness. But as the legendary Bruce Lee says, "Mistakes are always forgivable, if one has the courage to admit them."

CHAPTER 12
Trump vs. Trump

Divorce is a game played by lawyers.
Cary Grant

Love is supreme in human experience, hatred is self-consuming, and the distance between the two is one shockingly fine line.

Weddings are shared pledges of deep and permanent love between a husband and wife who adore one another. And yet the time may come, in the context of divorce, when an all-out, scorched-earth battle is carried about between those same two people. For friends who loved them both, it's distressing and confounding. How could this loving couple have come to this stage of mutual loathing?

We see it over and over. I've witnessed it far too often, given my line of work, and I would venture that you've observed your share of these awful scenes. The divorce papers are served—another function of my job description—and everything changes. "If you're not for me, you're against me," both partners decide. And suddenly, the stakes are too high for either party to simply walk away peacefully. There could be children, property, or just the public reputation of who was at fault.

Some divorcing husbands or wives are driven by long-suppressed resentment and rage. Divorce is Payback Time. On other occasions, the papers are served in the manner of Pearl Harbor—a surprise attack. The one served never saw it coming, copes with shock, then moves to the anger stage, then grief. There is such a thing as the no-fault divorce, where everyone remains friends, shakes hands, and moves on—but most divorces are terrible ordeals, clouds with no silver linings other than for the lawyers.

So hypothetically, if Melania Trump and Donald Trump are ever issued a court docket number, then it will be the most high-profile divorce in American history. A Trump vs. Trump scenario would reverberate worldwide. Scintillating media headlines would most likely describe a Trump civil proceeding that results in criminal punishment. Why? Exes are often encouraged by attorneys, judges, and court-appointed therapists to disclose the misdeeds of their significant other. The accuracy of the disclosures particularly coated in so much negative emotion has variable relationships to the truth. But once details such as a prior arrest, past alcohol abuse, previous drug use, or in Donald Trump's case alleged affairs are mentioned, then things become serious. Character assassination ensues.

What constitutes the most significant degree of fraud? Start with disclosures, or lack thereof, during divorce litigation. Willing and wanton acts of fraud include accruing excessive legal costs, hiding assets, defamation of character, parental alienation, and disproportionate child custody arrangements. Integrity goes out the window when it's all about what you're going to have left to build your life around—or just "sticking it to" someone you believe ruined your life.

The family law judge controls the disclosures above, along with which witnesses and evidence are admitted. The actual parties to the divorce do play a role in litigation, but judges ultimately make all the decisions and have all the power.

They're also very human, and if you rub a judge the wrong way, the impact on your future could be quite significant. This judge is what the pit boss is in a gambling casino—he or she presides over your future assets, your ability to see your children, and other factors incredibly important to you. This is why your attorney will be extremely anxious to discover which local judge is hearing a case. They're not all "created equal."

•••••••••●•••••••••

If, hypothetically, Melania contemplates divorce, naturally enough, she thinks about the immediate "costs" of leaving the marriage—the requirements of starting a new life, dealing with her child, social fallout,

IF THE FIRST LADY HIRED ME...

and the like. These are important things, of course. But there are financial costs that more often than not prove shocking to those who begin the long, litigious battle.

Attorneys, forensic accountants, court-appointed therapists, child psychologists, witnesses, and judges don't come cheap, and some or all of these may be involved. These are all part of the landscape of American family law that has developed, as divorce has become a vast industry. Many of these are distinguished people who care about their work, and I've known many good ones in all those categories. But I'll be fully honest. Lawyers and judges, in my experienced opinion, carry a great deal of blame for prolonging and complicating the litigation process of divorce.

Donald Trump is no stranger to lawsuits and the process of divorce proceedings. Of the more than 4,000 lawsuits Donald Trump has been involved in, his previous two divorces to Ivana Trump and Marla Maples proved costly. Both divorces mostly followed a prenuptial agreement; however, Ivana Trump contested the prenup and reportedly got $14 million, a sprawling mansion, a high-rise NYC apartment, as well as $650,000 per year for child support and alimony. Marla Maples contested the prenup between her and Donald too, but the award she received is undisclosed.

But if a high-stakes Melania Trump vs. Donald Trump divorce were to occur, then it's safe to say high profile attorneys will be in line to represent Melania ready to contest their prenup. Though it is difficult to overturn a prenup in New York, Melina's attorney could contend that she did not anticipate her husband would be President of the United States. Her attorney may request higher spousal support due to the fact she will incur more expenses as the first lady. All jewelry and personal items would most likely remain hers. Further, in order for the divorce not to see the light of day in a courtroom, Donald Trump may be willing to up the award to Melania.

If her divorce attorney is honest and caring, he might sit down with her at some point and say, "Let me give you a good idea of what's ahead, how much time it will involve, and how the costs are going to mount up." You need to factor in months (if not years) of anxiety, how all of it will affect your child and other factors such as the rest of your life.

A wise man said, "Never go to court over a principle." This isn't a simple matter of winning an argument. There are too many other factors involved, including your mental and emotional health and those of your children. This is a time when you need to think as clearly as possible and have the wisest possible advice from those who care about your and those who understand the future landscape. And it's a time when you need to be willing to take that advice.

> Let's do the math.
> The average length of divorce in America is ten months.
> Most divorce attorneys charge $200 to $500 per hour.
> Final tab: Perhaps $15,000 to $50,000. Final result: Divorce.

For those of us whose last name isn't Trump, should divorce really be that expensive? In the "fog of war," should couples be willing to pull out their wallets and pay out that kind of money?

Child support, alimony, expert witness fees such as those I've named, and division of debt and property are part of the process. Weeks pass, negotiations go back and forth like volleys of ammunition on the battlefield, and meanwhile, your attorney's meter continues to run. It's certainly no inconvenience to them; they have nothing to lose and everything to gain by litigating a lengthy divorce.

With such a great many marriages ending in divorce, it's safe to say that if you aren't divorced, you know someone who is. If you ever do contemplate severing the bond with your spouse, a smart thing to do would be to interview your friends who have been through it. How much money did it cost them? How much time? Were they satisfied with the process? You're likely to find that if they had it all to do over again, they'd find a way to get the same result, or something not too far from it, with far less time and financial expense. And it's nearly always possible.

Attorneys immediately advise their clients not to speak to their separated partners, but to put out the word that they should "talk to my attorney." This may be useful advice if, for example, emotions are too high for healthy communication. But sometimes, feelings cool down, and the two spouses might well wonder if they could only get together and work things out between themselves, thus saving a fortune in both time and money. With the lawyers in full control, however, all the apparatus of the divorce industry comes into play.

Mediation is a real option. If you or someone you know has less than $100,000 in assets, it deserves strong consideration. Why? You drastically slash the legal fees. You avoid your emotions (and your attorneys) writing an ever-larger check that your bank account can't pay.

Consider a more intangible quality, too: the emotional cost of litigation is costly in a different way. A skirmish becomes a war, the stakes keep getting higher, and whatever positive memories you might have had about your spouse and your marriage are gone forever. The whole process has caused emotional breakdowns for some people. It has set entire armies of friends on two opposing sides. It has left sad scars on the psyches of many children. There must be a better way.

The more money you have, of course, the smaller your chances of any kind of reasonable and straightforward divorce experience. For billionaires, the litigation can be of epic proportion and play out across the pages of the tabloids. That said, if a prenuptial agreement was not in place for Mr. and Mrs. Trump and a divorce ensued, then it could very well play out similar to Mr. and Mrs. Hamm's split. Harold Hamm is the name not of a cartoon character but an oil fracking billionaire.

Hamm divorced his wife in 2015. He offered a generous settlement, but the tycoon wasn't about to get off that easy. The just under a billion offer wasn't nearly enough to maintain her life with the comforts to which she was accustomed. She asked for more.

The case began in 2012, and eventually made it up the legal ladder to the Oklahoma Supreme Court by 2015. Mr. Hamm's ex-wife felt she was worthy of a few billion, and the two deadly battalions of uber-lawyers escalated the conflict. Certainly, there was "blood in the water" among the various expert witnesses and specialists. Ms. Hamm threw out charges of her husband's philandering.

After a two-month trial in 2015, she received a $975 million judgment, one of the largest ever in a U. S. divorce. (Bernie Ecclestone and Slavica Ecclestone settled for as much as $1.2 billion. Some readers may decide that while a divorce is too costly, becoming a divorce attorney is a career worth thinking about!)

The Hamm's were married for two decades, and all their ups

and downs, their differences and their foibles, were played out in the Oklahoma court system for years, at enormous expense. The size of your bank account tracks to the complexity and anguish of your divorce proceedings.

If there's any lesson to be learned, other than count the cost first—it's the necessity of prenuptial agreements. Did you think those are just for the wealthy? Think again.

•••••••••●••••••••••

Nobody considers a "prenup" to be very romantic when they pop the question and the future seems rosy. Preachers declare it to be a lack of faith in marriage and one another. But the truth is, we buy car insurance. We buy homeowner's insurance, and of course, we buy policies to cover our very lives. Why not a written policy to cover the destruction of a marriage? That's what the prenup does, and what it lacks in sentiment, it more than gains in saved expense and heartache later.

A prenuptial agreement provides clarity and conclusion in the event a marriage fails. The two partners in the struggling marriage have an exit strategy. They know that should they decide to go their separate ways; the terms will be all set out. There's not much to litigate. A lot of "sound and fury, signifying nothing," in Shakespeare's words, will be spared. No one suffers but perhaps a hungry lawyer, if such a thing exists.

Should you consider a prenup? How would you go about getting one?

First, explain the sensible reasons for it to your bride or groom-to-be. Again, it's not a discussion anyone would enjoy, but given the fact that nobody anticipates a divorce, yet unfortunately too many marriages end in divorce—wise partners will take wise precautions.

Talk about what's fair financially. Work out custodial arrangements if children are involved. Naturally, each party will make concessions and establish priorities, but work out everything you can *before* meeting with an attorney. As discussed earlier, attorneys often muddy the water and can legally complicate an understanding between couples.

Note carefully: Each party needs to be represented by different attorneys to prevent a conflict of interest. It's a matter of practicality and not the rehearsal of an actual divorce. As a matter of fact, speaking frankly and planning the future is healthy for any marriage. The prenup should be descriptive in nature and be in effect for a set period of time (five or seven years from signing is typical). The agreement needs to be signed and notarized to be binding.

When those five to seven years approach their close, what should you do? Obtain a *post*nuptial agreement, and simply use the same methodology. This new agreement will take precedence over the prenup.

• • • • • • • • • • ● • • • • • • • • • • •

The American family law system is tailor-made for divorce lawyers to line their pockets. Issues of child custody, spousal support, and asset division can be prolonged, and the meter continues to run. Litigants foot the bill. Any conflict and confusion raise the heat, tempting the two parties to double down on their stubbornness to win at all costs. Good common sense, cooler heads, and mediation would help, but the more the assets, the less likely that people will choose this route.

We also should note that the litigants themselves can be a big part of the problems. Plenty of fraud goes on during divorce cases. Assets are hidden or moved. Income is misrepresented. There may even be fabricated accusations of spousal abuse, or, just as effective, the threats of these which can destroy someone's good name. Friends and loved ones watch from the sidelines and wonder how things ever came to this.

Asset concealment can be accomplished by transferring property from one's name to that of an accomplice—a friend or family member. Large sums of money, jewelry, and other valuables can be stored in a safe deposit box titled to someone else, where no inventory will find them. Or when emotions run so high as to be irrationally devious, someone may use the idea of fund dissipation—the destruction of marital property, excessive spending of assets, gambling, or selling assets for less than they're worth. It's really just another form of fraud, but it's quite common.

Some of these ideas may be entirely new to you. But everyone who enters the honorable institution of wedlock needs at least a quick course on the nature of divorce litigation. It's shocking, and none of us expect it to ever happen to us. But divorces are incredibly common at every level of society, and you need to know the facts before too quickly embracing the idea that divorce court is the best way to go. Almost any other course (other than such things as staying in an abusive marriage) is preferable.

•••••••••●•••••••••

New Hampshire is the best state for getting a divorce—followed by Wyoming, then Alaska. It can be done quickly and inexpensively. In fact, you can move there, say, from Massachusetts (120 days to process the paperwork) and quickly get a divorce the next day. There's no minimum residency period. If you live in Vermont, ranked by Bloomberg in 2011 as the worst place to dissolve a marriage, you'll want to move temporarily to New Hampshire. In Vermont, six months of separation are required by law, and if you haven't lived in Vermont for at least a year, you're ineligible for a divorce anyway.

The states all have specific divorce laws, policies, and restrictions. You'll want to do a little research (and you can do that on the Internet without hiring a divorce attorney to explain it to you). Only New Hampshire, Wyoming, and Alaska have discounted divorces, so I'll close this chapter by offering you a few wallet-friendly alternatives.

Alternative 1. Mediation

In mediation, a third party, who is neutral, comes alongside the couple to facilitate negotiations. The mediator helps make communication easier between the two sides but isn't empowered to render any decisions.

Attorneys can be consulted before and after the mediation, primarily to review the settlement agreement prior to signing. But their fee will be a small fraction of what it would be for full-scale litigation.

Alternative 2. Arbitration

In arbitration, there is also a third party who is neutral. In this case, however, he or she listens carefully to both sides, examines all the known facts, and deliberates toward a final decision. As would happen in court, the divorcing spouses present their evidence, argue, and defend their position, but the arbitrator maintains orderly proceedings and will have the final say in the decision rendered.

On the positive side, both mediation and arbitration:

- Reduce the cost of divorce.
- Establish privacy rather than a public, litigated divorce.
- Expedite the process, allowing for a quicker resolution.
- Are better all-around for the children.

On the negative side, these two options:

- Fail to uncover assets which are not volunteered by both parties.
- May end in a settlement that can't be enforced over time.
- May make relations and matters worse between spouses.

Alternative 3: Collaborative Divorce

The newest method and alternative for resolution is *collaborative divorce*. This approach, using mediation and negotiation, is designed to avoid the bitter disputes that divorce so often entail. In collaborative divorce, no litigation is allowed between divorcing spouses and their attorneys. Various cooperative techniques help avoid conflict and a battle overflowing into the courtroom.

Again, all parties must agree from the outset to honor the terms that are brought about during the negotiations. It's a viable alternative, and in fact, many courts are now requiring that mediation or collaborative divorce be tried before courtroom litigation is allowed. The divorce industry may not favor that, but it's healthy for the public at large.

Think of some of the sadder divorce stories you've observed. A family law judge rules against a parent. Assets are divided in a way that one side resents. Custody may be denied. Whether the ruling is fair or not isn't the issue. The real problem is that families are destroyed by the bitterness that is created. The two divorcing spouses have no real chance at keeping any kind of civil relationship going forward. This is terribly destructive to children, and for that matter, to the happiness of the two parties.

CHAPTER 13
Cheating is the Kiss of Death...

"Cheaters never win and winners never cheat."
Andrew Keane

I won't deny that one particular form of cheating and dishonor has become my particular focus. As someone whose young life was devastated by infidelity, I've delved deeper into that part of life, not simply to punish it, but because I want to understand its root causes.

My work as a private investigator has given me the opportunity to interview and consult with dozens of adulterers over a ten-year period. I've come into contact with cheaters of every race, creed, sexual preference, and socioeconomic background. There are many kinds of people, but our problems are universal, and the reasons we step away from relationship commitments are ultimately predictable.

To help me understand, I've attended marriage conferences, spoken with psychologists, consulted with pastors, and read page after page of marriage manuals and analyses. Having done all this and reflecting deeply, I've developed an idea of my own about why people cheat.

First, in explaining infidelity, theory and practice are separate matters. A marriage counselor or a pastor will have certain ideas, but mine may vary after watching through parted curtains and a surveillance camera. The lens shows me not what people say, but what they do. Instead of beginning with statistics or psychology profiles, my starting point is the actions of individuals. That is, I work from the bottom up, behavior to theory, instead of the other way around.

Sherlock Holmes, also a private investigator (if a fictional one), shared my experience. He says: "It is a capital mistake to theorize before one has data. Insensibly one begins to twist facts to suit theories, instead of theories to suit facts."

A theorist might speak of socioeconomic factors, psychological factors, or the spiritual corruption of the soul. For me, it boils down to one word: *selfishness*. The more people are prone to put themselves first, the more likely they are to cheat.

Why is this significant? My perspective gives me less rosy hopes for the future of marriages and monogamous relationships disrupted by unfaithfulness. Theorists write action plans for "working out differences," practicing radical forgiveness, and the like. On paper, it all adds up to a pretty picture of redemption and restoration. It sells books; it makes for uplifting sermons.

In practice, however, it's just not what I've observed.

I've seen real affairs rather than theoretical ones. I've observed the power of true hurt and betrayal, soul-deep. "Happily ever after" is a phrase we've drawn from fairy tales, but for damaged marriages, it very rarely applies. I've made it a point to share a chapter about "divine intervention" as my client described it because I want to stress there are always outliers. I would advise no one to simply abandon hope. But again—the truth is always my north star. I let it guide me even when it doesn't tell the story people want to hear.

The inconvenient fact is that those who have cheated once are the most at risk to cheat again—even when they've shown remorse; even when they've attended helpful counseling, seen the pain their spouses and children felt, and all these things. What made them cheat is something deep within, and it's still there.

> Not that I traffic in psychobabble. I have no interest in categorizing cheaters as sex addicts, sociopaths, or sinners. I hold to the term SELFISHNESS, and that's a deep-rooted personality trait. The most unselfish people

I know have always been who they are, and the reverse is also true. Cheaters are prone to cheat.

· · · · · · · · · ● · · · · · · · · · ·

For the special purpose of this book, I questioned fifty spouses who have cheated, and I was struck again and again by their candor. This was a group that cut across the socioeconomic spectrum. There were successful businessmen and doctors, sturdy blue-collar workers, millennial techies, and others, and no matter what their background, they were ready, even eager to honestly share their experiences in philandering. Whether in past or present marriages, all had been involved in adultery.

As I heard all these stories, each one unforgettable in its own way—how could a story of bitter betrayal not be? — I found my interviews taking the new form of a broader pursuit of the truth behind marriage breakdowns. What were the causes of cheating? What were the effects? In each case, I gave my assurance of confidentiality, and of course, I'll honor it. Names and specific details have been altered to protect the privacy of these people.

Those familiar, broad statistics were never my goal or any significant part of my method. I wanted genuine human experience because none of us are statistics. Every one of us has a story that differs from every other. Each person, each marriage is an only partly open book that would be as gripping as a bestselling thriller if all the details were honestly shared.

So I went for those details instead of categorizing people into statistical templates. A case study of fifty cheaters is too small a sample for drawing any broad picture anyway. But fifty is enough that an interviewer can begin to recognize and identify recurring patterns of failure, response, emotion. I'm convinced that if I interviewed five hundred instead of fifty, I'd come to the same conclusion—namely the following:

> *Theory: Only twenty-two percent of couples, having gone through the crisis of cheating, will remain happily married.*

My interviews revealed that thirty-nine of the fifty spouses were divorced, separated, or unhappily married as a result of extramarital affairs. Not surprisingly, the 78 percent of divorce, separated, or unhappily married spouses blamed infidelity as the root cause for the demise of their marriage. Over and over, I heard words to the effect of, "Without trust, what do you have?" That was the recurring summary of the whole experience.

Forty-eight people (96 percent) admitted to cheating on their spouse more than once.

All (100 percent) admitted to lying and attempting to cover-up the affair.

With whom do people cheat? Of those I interviewed, the genesis of several affairs occurred online, but most often the affairs were "hidden in plain sight." They occurred with friends or co-workers, right beneath the spouse's nose.

Most remarkable of all, all fifty cheaters (100 percent) freely admitted that the root cause of their infidelity was selfishness. How did I come to that conclusion? I asked the same two questions to each cheater, "During the affair, did your own <u>want</u> for sexuality supersede your spouse's <u>need</u> for monogamy? If so, would you describe that behavior as selfish?"

All responded, "Yes."

You can begin to see why I don't feel the need to interview hundreds of other cheaters. When fifty out of fifty people point to one specific cause of an action that disrupted other lives, the pattern is clear enough.

Selfishness, we might agree, is also a sin that hides in plain sight. It's the cause of all human failure. And nobody is truly innocent of self-centered behavior. But it's possible that two people, considering marriage and wondering, "Will he/she cheat?" might begin with the question of selfishness. Why? A great deal of selfishness is required to enable someone to act for personal, momentary pleasure in a way that is so hurtful to a spouse, to children, to friends.

Indeed, the ripple effect of an affair is worth considering. What about the children? What about the hurt experienced by the extended family, a church community, business relationships, a circle of friends? No man (or woman) is an island.

Every cheater I interviewed was negatively impacted personally, of course. They hurt themselves by damaging children, family, finances, friends, co-workers, church, and even future partners who will have to deal with more blowback than either of them anticipates. Emotions leave wounds, including guilt, which lasts far longer than people expect. Waves of regret and guilt will resurface for years, long after the time of the storm.

But surely there's some ray of hope. What about the fortunate eleven—those I interviewed who are somehow still married—even, they insist, "happily"? They're making it work, but they also express an inability to trust their marriage partner fully. They admit to keeping that spouse on a short leash, just to be sure. We also have to take into account factors such as religious belief. As previously discussed, whether or not a marriage can be restored through "so-called" divine intervention is, of course, possible but not probable.

Such improbability of restoring trust takes shape due to the vast majority of those cheated on opt out of the relationship. This assertion as evidenced by the Twittersphere's overwhelming response to my @ Justin_Hopson poll in 2018—where 505 anonymous users voted:

- *If cheated on, you leave*   87%
- *If cheated on, you stay?*   13%

But there is one looming question that should be the baseline for anyone tempted to cheat. The success of life itself might hinge on the ability of someone to ask it and answer it honestly: Are the "rewards" of an affair—the pleasure, the thrill, the breaking of life's monotony—worth the risks? Are they worth the full price, which always comes due later?

· · · · · · · · · ● · · · · · · · · · ·

Maybe I still have a little of the old state trooper in me: With this book, I'm posting a *no trespassing* sign to potential cheaters, and on the other side of the road, a *detour* sign to those who have been cheated upon. Yet I learned in that previous career how seriously people take traffic signs.

I've found that the process of writing this book has only intensified my desire to speak out on an issue that is destroying too many families. I hope you'll put a copy of this volume into the hands of your friends and family, whether you think they need it or not. I want to start a nationwide conversation about the epidemic of cheating and to create a new passion for protecting our marriages and relationships, which are the nurturing places for our children and the center of our wellbeing.

Much as I want to see all monogamous relationships protected, my most sensible advice to those who have been cheated upon is to walk away. The laws of probability are not in your favor, in terms of avoiding future pain. The first cut is the deepest, but future cuts will do even more considerable damage to your chances of happiness.

If you walk away after the first offense, even then, you must be patient with the healing process. It may take many months, even years. But you have a chance to start over, and many, many good opportunities will come with that, even as you do your grief work and learn to master the anger and resentment you've taken with you. New life is possible. But if you double down and recommit to life with a cheater, you can lose your sense of self over time. You may find you've drifted into a life of quiet desperation and gloom.

Some will read this and say, "It can't be this black and white. People do change. Life has gray areas."

I would argue that cheating is a black and white proposition. Unfaithfulness is such a long, swaggering step over the line that it tells the most revealing story about that person. The whole basis of a committed relationship is trust.

Virginity can't be reacquired once it's lost, and I would argue that trust in relationships is the same way. Sure, if you do work through it somehow, if the cheater is truly a "sadder but wiser" mate, and all the pieces are taped back together, that's a great story, even inspiring. But have you thought about what you'll be putting yourself through the first time he doesn't come home on time from work? The time he seems to panic when you pick up his phone? The occasion at the office Christmas party when you can't help but watch how he looks at other women? Will your sex life truly be the same, and what will you think when he seems to lose interest?

Let me tell you what will happen. You'll be reminded of the way you felt before when you first found out he (or she) was cheating—do you want to face that again? The deep, empty pang in the pit of your stomach? The anxiety attacks? The dulled shock, shame, and the periods of deep depression? We weren't made to go through this once, but to allow it to happen again is madness.

I've simply watched too many real-life case studies and know what a restless imagination can do to people who have been hurt. I understand that broken trust doesn't quickly repair itself. A clean break may seem cold and unforgiving, but in real life, it's the best hope.

They say, "Forgive and forget." Have you ever noticed that we can do the first part of that (difficult as it is), but never the second part? Try forgetting the worst thing that ever happened to you. Certain kinds of pain engrave themselves on the soul. And here's the kicker. We can fool ourselves into thinking we've "completely forgiven," but forgiveness is partially based on a certain level of forgetting—which we can't do. So, forgive? Maybe; very, very difficult. Forget? Forget it!

Faith-based approaches are useful, but we're still only human. Counseling has its place, but there's no surgery, no procedure that can reach into the depths of a scarred soul and mind.

I've expressed my share of bemusement over statistics, and I feel the same way about theoretical approaches to this issue, even as someone who studied psychology in college. My best education has been in the school of human experience, where people are simply people. They are as they act, and the surveillance camera doesn't lie.

Last but not least, let me reiterate some practical advice to this book's namesake—First Lady, Melania Trump.

I hope your life provides you with peace of mind and stillness of heart. Honesty, forgiveness, and unconditional love are part of that equation. If the one closest to you isn't honest, then it may be time to begin again. Yes, I said it. Start anew, and let the lawyers handle the formalities.

Melania, as for public opinion it doesn't matter, but I'd venture to say you'll be held in high esteem. No longer cast as the ice-princess by the media, rather a matriarch for monogamy and a role model for those victimized by cheating. Whatever decision you make just remember that *cheating IS the kiss of death to marriage and monogamous relationships.*

Stay faithful, my friends, and stay hopeful, Melania.

Also from Justin Hopson

Breaking the Blue Wall
One Man's War Against Police Corruption

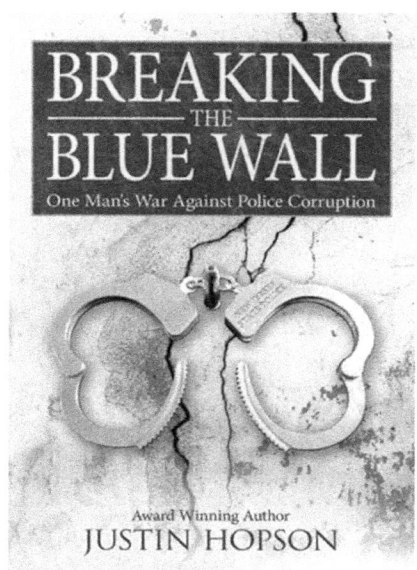

With only eleven days on the job as a rookie New Jersey State Trooper, Justin Hopson witnessed an act of police corruption.

When Trooper Hopson refused to testify in support of the illegal arrest; his life veered into a dangerous journey of harassment and retaliation. Fear, paranoia, and depression overtook Trooper Hopson as he was victimized by a secret society within the state police known as the Lords of Discipline.

For decades the Lords of Discipline (LOD) hazed and bullied fellow troopers in order to keep them in line and in fear of speaking out against police impropriety. But then the Lords targeted someone willing to put his career and life on the line to unearth wrongdoing. Trooper Hopson blew the whistle on the Lords of Discipline, sparking the largest internal investigation in state police history and high-profile federal case.

Justin Hopson's true crime memoir takes you behind law enforcement's "blue wall of silence" and discloses his harrowing journey of exposing police corruption and living to tell about it. This compelling book is a modern day *Serpico*, one where an ordinary cop with an extraordinary cause defies the odds and dangers of blowing the whistle on police corruption, brutality, and hazing.

Justin Hopson's efforts have been recognized and supported by Frank

Serpico (NYPD), Senator John Adler, The National Whistleblower Center, Jane Turner (FBI), and Dr. Susan Lipkins. In addition, Mr. Hopson has been interviewed and featured by ABC News, The New York Times, The Philadelphia Inquirer, Lowcountry Live, The Star-Ledger, and 20/20. "Breaking the Blue Wall is a very cool book and a great read," Tom Crawford (ABC).

Order your copy of Justin Hopson's award-winning story today.

AVAILABLE FROM AMAZON OR ORDER
FROM - JUSTINHOPSON.COM

Notes

Chapter 3: Private Eye 101

<u>Source</u>: "New Private Investigative Business License" *SLED online;* Revised 7/2017; *http://www.sled.sc.gov/Documents/PI/pilicnew.pdf*

Chapter 5: You Do the Math

Matthew 19:9
Malachi 2:16

Chapter 11: Divine Intervention

1 Peter 4:8

About the Author

Award winning author, Justin Hopson, is a seasoned private investigator and served as a New Jersey State Trooper before retiring in 2007. Mr. Hopson has been a interviewed and featured on ABC News 20/20, The New York Times, The Philadelphia Inquirer, The Star-Ledger, Bloomberg News, and Progressive Radio. His efforts to unearth corruption have been supported by the likes of Frank Serpico, Senator John Adler, Dr. Susan Lipkins, and the National Whistleblower Center.

Justin Hopson has successfully testified in federal, state, and municipal court proceedings. He was appointed to the Charleston County Alcohol and Drug Abuse Advisory Board and the South Carolina Association of Legal Investigator's Ethics Committee. His presentations and book signing events have been hosted by The Military Order of World Wars, Auburn University's Anti-Bullying Summit, South Carolina Association of Legal Investigators, business conferences, universities, churches, and community centers nationwide.

www.ingramcontent.com/pod-product-compliance
Lightning Source LLC
LaVergne TN
LVHW041628070426
835507LV00008B/514